Tradition
for Crisis

A Study in Hosea

Walter Brueggemann

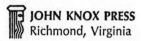 JOHN KNOX PRESS
Richmond, Virginia

With the exception of occasional translations by the author, Scripture quotations are from the *Revised Standard Version of the Bible,* copyrighted 1946 and 1952.

LIBRARY OF CONGRESS CATALOG CARD NUMBER: 68-21008

© M. E. BRATCHER 1968

PRINTED IN THE UNITED STATES OF AMERICA

22-0180

for Mary

Contents

Tradition and Crisis:
A Study in Prophetic Ministry

Current polarization in the church will no doubt get worse before it gets better. The gap gets wider and wider between those who want the church involved in the issues of the day and those who cherish the traditional forms and formulations. Conflict of this kind is not unhealthy if it is in the service of the church's ministry and mission, but the contemporary conflict has now advanced until it is not grounded in our ministry but in the defense of positions. Its mood is not one of fidelity to our mission but one of distrust and acrimony.

This study addresses itself to this unfortunate and unhealthy polarization. It explores the meaning of prophecy as the basis of our problem and also as a resource by which we may deal with it constructively. Recent developments in the study of Israel's prophets have brought significant changes in our understanding of them and in the discernment of our role as heirs of the prophets. New methods of interpretation and fresh presuppositions lead us to a new appreciation of the prophetic quality of Biblical faith and therefore of the ministry of that prophetic community today. I have selected Hosea as the basis for study because he more than anyone in ancient Israel (with the possible exception of Jeremiah) experienced in his own life the polarization which is now wrenching the church. None understood the faith of the fathers more clearly than he or took it more seriously. None was more involved in and troubled by his contemporary situation. The anguish and pathos of his tradition are a model for the same anguish and pathos which many feel today about the church as it struggles to maintain unity and yet embody some measure of purity.

I have also wanted to keep in mind current ecumenical discussions concerning Scripture and tradition. Ancient Israel understood the relation between past tradition and present crisis in ways which have important implications for our own understanding of a live and authoritative tradition. The prophetic quality of tradition is being rediscovered by Roman Catholics in amazing ways. And

11

we Protestants struggle with this same prophetic dimension that seems not to go away. We want very much to be sons and daughters of the sixteenth-century disturbers, but we are less sure about wanting to be disturbed in our own time and place. I know of no way which helps us get at this so inescapably as listening again to the disturbance which came upon Israel in the prophets.

Polarization in the church between conservatives and liberals, new understanding of the prophets and new methods of Bible study, new insight into Scripture and tradition are, however, all subordinate questions. The great question which concerns this book and which must be continually before us all is the relevance of the Biblical tradition for our kind of world. Does it make sense any longer to think about meaning in history as we have conventionally done? This study hopes at least to clarify that question which looms so large in contemporary discussion.

Along the way it is also true that we lack an introduction in English to contemporary prophetic study. This book has grown out of frustration in having nowhere to send students for an exposure to fresh scholarship. The text and notes are an attempt in this direction.

The present study is indebted to all sorts of people for a variety of reasons. First stands the name of Professor James Muilenburg, whose influence is pervasive and apparent to those who know him. Obviously my approach is shaped and guided by the work of Gerhard von Rad. I have been helped greatly by my colleagues at Eden Seminary, Eugene Wehrli and Lionel Whiston, Jr., and especially by Richard L. Scheef, Jr., who has made many helpful suggestions for my study. In a quite different way I am beholden to members at Central Presbyterian Church in St. Louis who have struggled with me in the question of tradition and crisis. The book is dedicated to my wife Mary with gratitude, for with her I have learned much about the wrestlings reflected in this book.

Walter Brueggemann
Eden Seminary
St. Louis, Missouri
September 1, 1967

I.

The Covenant Context
of the Prophets of Israel[1]

A central fact in the study of the eighth-century prophets of the Old Testament has come clear in recent times. The prophets can only be understood in the context of the ancient historical and legal traditions of the Pentateuch. Several generations of scholarship (and therefore of the church) have assumed that there is a sharp discontinuity between the religion of the Torah and the faith of the prophets, that the prophets represent a phenomenon which is radically new and which can be understood in relation to the Torah only by means of contrast. This assumption grows out of the notion that the ethical religion of the prophets is superior to the cultic religion of the Torah, that monotheism in the prophets has superseded the polytheism of the Torah, and that individualism in the prophets is superior to the collectivism of the Torah. This means that we need not begin with the Torah but can come to the prophets and understand them fully on their own terms.

The new direction of scholarship, which is not the movement of any special school or tradition of scholars, makes it clear beyond doubt that we can understand the prophets only in relation to the old historical and legal traditions preserved in the Torah. The prophets have as their primary function the reassertion and application of the old traditions in ways which are relevant and compelling for the present community of faith. They do not invent new ideas to speak nor are they mere repeaters of the old traditions. But their words and acts are thoroughly grounded in the ancient faith which has its source in Moses. The prophets are concerned to establish points of contact between (a) the faith of the community as it has been formulated in previous times and (b) the present

13

situation of the community in its various historical circumstances. To do this, they handle the old traditions creatively but faithfully.[2]

For the study of the prophets, this means that we must be thoroughly informed concerning the older traditions of the Torah before we can hope to understand the intention of the prophets. Before we can understand how the prophets apply the old traditions to the present situation, we must know these old traditions immediately. We must develop the tools to understand the traditions. We must enter into the faith of the old traditions and the worship life in which the traditions had their meaningful existence. Only then can we ask the question: how do the prophets appropriate these traditions for their own time?

For the present church in her prophetic ministry this poses new challenges. It has been widely assumed by theologians and preachers that the sermonizing of the church should be prophetic. It has been too easily assumed that the people of God are prepared to hear prophetic preaching. But this so-called prophetic preaching has in general been negative and judgmental, e.g., to admonish the church for having forsaken the faith of the fathers or having violated the commands of the tradition. This approach to prophetic preaching, however, has not been noticeably successful, and it becomes increasingly futile. The present church is by and large uninformed about her heritage of faith. She is largely unaware of the historical and legal traditions in the context of which she must theologize and live. Such preaching, then, becomes an attempt to address the present church in a prophetic way without her awareness of the traditions which stand behind a prophetic ministry. Thus, our ministry has been set in a vacuum.

In light of this, the present undertaking has a general interest in the study of the history of Old Testament faith, but also a specific concern for the life of the present church. I wish to suggest both to the student and to the churchman (and one person is often both), that we cannot address ourselves to prophetic faith nor be addressed by it until we have lived ourselves into the traditions which provide the necessary context for prophecy. This is true concerning both ancient Israel and the contemporary church. Specifically, we cannot summon or admonish the church until the church knows deeply what God has done for her (historical traditions) and what God has called her to do (legal traditions) in response.

Before turning to the prophets in a consideration of their relation to the ancient traditions, we must briefly give attention to those traditions which stand behind the prophets.

The Historical Traditions

Primarily through the work of Gerhard von Rad,[3] we may now say that the historical memory of Israel has its earliest and most succinct expression in the cultic confessions which are preserved for us in a liturgic form:

> "A wandering Aramean was my father; and he went down into Egypt and sojourned there, few in number; and there he became a nation, great, mighty, and populous. And the Egyptians treated us harshly, and afflicted us, and laid upon us hard bondage. Then we cried to the LORD the God of our fathers, and the LORD heard our voice, and saw our affliction, our toil, and our oppression; and the LORD brought us out of Egypt with a mighty hand and an outstretched arm, with great terror, with signs and wonders; and he brought us into this place and gave us this land, a land flowing with milk and honey. . . ." (Deut. 26:5-9).

It is now generally recognized that this statement contains the primary convictions by which Israel lived. The statement mentions only three memories: the wandering of the fathers, here specifically Jacob; the rescue from slavery in Egypt; and the entrance into the promised land. The first and the third of these belong together as promise and fulfillment. God makes his promise to the fathers and fulfills it in the conquest under Joshua. The second point, which is really the center of the confession, gives vitality and power to the other two. It is because of this great victory that Israel dares to trust in the promise to the fathers and can see in the land-entrance the fulfillment of the promise by God.

Several factors about these statements might be noted. First, they are very brief and to the point. They are not attempts to argue, explain, or prove anything. They are confessions by the believing community in the context of faith. They make no appeal to those who do not or cannot believe. The statements assume that the speaker and the hearer share the confession. Second, there are only three events named. The confession is very limited and selective. This is not a narrative about the total memory of the people but only a recital of the great crisis events which have helped to determine the destiny and character of life. This is not a haphazard statement but is canonical, i.e., normative for all of life. Third, the statements remember historical events, happenings in the experience of the community. There is nothing in this affirmation of faith about theological or eternal truths or propositions which must be believed. They are only memories about events in "our" past. Fourth, they all concern something God has done for Israel. There is nothing here about what Israel has done or must do. In Israel's affirmation of faith and her confession about reality, human effort is never primary. Israel stakes her life on the confession that this God acts for her in ways which save her and make life good.

When Israel has confessed this faith, she has made her basic affirmation about the nature of reality and about the character of her own life. Israel understands herself as being the object, recipient, and beneficiary of the gracious sovereign actions of God. She is not one who makes history but one for whom God does history. Her memory reminds her that her destiny in life is to respond fully and faithfully to these actions.

God is known in terms of what he has done for his special people. This basic affirmation is expanded to include other dimensions of the experience of the community, but these do not alter the basic character and primary place of the credo as we have suggested it.[4] Additional data only support the fundamental response Israel makes to this history-making God.

Israel affirmed that God led her for many years in the wilderness, when she was very insecure and much in need, when she had no support for life but to trust God (Pss. 105:39-41; 136:16). This is a confession by the community that God is faithful and can be relied upon to care for his people, which at times is a fickle people.[5] Israel's major role in this tradition is to "murmur" (Ps. 106:25), i.e., to protest against God. This is a refusal to accept the place where God called her to be (Exod. 16-17). In some ways this is a minor motif in the tradition, and serves in the whole story primarily to move the people from one locus of action (Egypt) to the next one (Canaan). But it is more than a device for transition. It is also a significant affirmation of faith.

Another basic element in the tradition is the memory of the covenant at Sinai/Horeb (Neh. 9:13-15). Whether or not this was originally joined to the Exodus event is much disputed among scholars. We here assume that it was original, for without it, Israel's memory would not have been what it was. This tradition places more emphasis upon the action of Israel than the others which stress the deeds of the Lord. But even here, the covenant may be understood as a manifestation of his graciousness. In the Exodus event God had indicated in a very forceful way that he wished Israel to be his special people in an intimate and unique relation with him. In the Sinai tradition the Lord makes special provision for the continuation and consolidation of this special relation initiated by the miraculous saving deed of the Exodus. Election has its continuation in covenant. God's initiating act is free and unconditional. But if the relation is to continue, then certain conditions and responsibility for the relation must be delineated. The covenant of Sinai, which is remembered in this tradition, is an attempt to stabilize and guarantee this relation which God so graciously offered to Israel (Exod. 19-24).

In the tenth century, the time of David and Solomon, this faith in a jealous God who chooses a special people for his own receives mature reflection. There is an attempt made by very sophisticated theologians to interpret this special relation in the inclusive scope of the entire creation. The question must be asked, what is the meaning of this covenant for God's relation to the rest of the world? To probe this question, Israel's faith reflects upon the meaning of creation and God's purpose for the world which he has made (Ps. 136:4-9). In the more extended forms of the credo, the faith which begins with the promise to Abraham stands in the larger context of God's intention for his whole world (Neh. 9:6-8). The God who saves us is the same God who made the whole world! Or to invert it as Israel would do: the God who made the world is none other than the one who meets us as Savior (Gen. 2-11).[6]

Finally, also in the tenth century, the phenomenon of monarchy arose in Israel because of the pressure of the Philistines. Kingship was not germane to the oldest faith of Israel and there was considerable question about its legitimacy. But it did in fact assume a central position in the life of Israel. For the relevance of the credo, this new fact had also to be interpreted as a gracious historical deed of Yahweh (Ps. 78:67-72). So in the credo of the tenth century, the Davidic establishment is presented as the culmination of the normative confession of faith in Israel. What had been in the earliest confessions only a sketchy memory about the most important crises becomes in the tenth century a sweeping and inclusive statement which moves from God's plan for history to the dynasty of David (see Ps. 78).[7]

This confession of historical deeds was in the tenth century and thereafter expressed in eloquent narrative form, gathering to itself a variety of materials to explore the various dimensions of this history. We now have that completed narrative development of the creedal affirmation:

Gen. 1-11	God's intention for the world: creation
Gen. 12-50	God's promise to Israel: the fathers
Exod. 1-15	God's elective love for Israel: the Exodus
Exod. 16-18; Num. 10-36	God's faithful leadership: the Sojourn
Exod. 19—Num. 10	God's covenant with Israel: the law of Sinai
Joshua 1-12	God's fulfillment of his promise: the gift of the land
1 Sam.; 2 Sam. 1-7	The later Southern development of the Davidic establishment as God's final ordering for Israel[8]

Two aspects of this must be held in close relation to each other: (a) This is, as we now have it, narrative form which had a long history and a fairly free pattern of growth and development. (b) The roots of this narrative pattern are not in the mind of an author, nor in events as they were accidentally remembered, but in the public confession of faith which was made normative through its liturgic use. The historical traditions have their primary and normative existence in the public liturgy where all Israel came periodically to confess her faith in this God. Modification of this liturgic material is caused by an urgent need to accommodate new historical contexts.

In the following chapters of this presentation we will want to consider the relation of the prophets to these traditions. Our analysis will seek to show (a) that the prophets remembered these traditions and that their whole message depended upon them and (b) that they not only remembered the traditions but reformulated them in ways to make them relevant for the contemporary circumstance. In the hands of the prophets as also in the liturgy of Israel, the traditions cease to be only memories of the past and become important tools or weapons for the present moment of faith.[9]

The Legal Traditions

While the center of the ancient traditions is found in the historical memories of what God has done, there is a significant body of material which is concerned with "law." The election love of God needed to be consolidated, and this required a response on the part of Israel. This is the Lord's command to the community: "If you would live in relation with me, this is what you must do. . . ." (see Deut. 30:15-20). We have violated the real character of this material by referring to it as "law," for that is not what it is. It is rather "Torah," i.e., the direction the covenant Lord gives to his covenant people. There is nothing in it of the abstract and rationalistic notion of law, so that we would do well not to translate the word but to leave it simply "Torah."

This material, which includes Exodus 20:1-17 (the Ten Commandments), Exodus 21:1—23:19 (the Covenant Code), Exodus 25-31, 35-40, Leviticus, and Numbers 1-10 (the Priestly Code which includes the Holiness Code [Lev. 18-26]), is diverse in its form and content, so that it is impossible to find a clear pattern or structure in it.[10] Moreover, the legal heritage of the ancient Near

East as known in the law codes going back to 2000 B.C. shows that Israel did extensive borrowing. This makes the problem more acute when we seek to discern what is "authentically Israelite."

What is new in these materials and unique to Israel is that the legal traditions are brought into close and decisive relationship with this God and his spokesman, Moses. These are not any longer laws or rules for the ordering of the cult or society generally, but they are offered as the will of God for his people. They are conditions for a continuing relation which have their origin in the will of the covenant Lord. Though they cover a variety of subjects, they have as their single intention to bring all of life under the immediate, direct, and radical lordship of this God. No area of life is free from his purpose and his will. Therefore, in these laws no area of life is excluded from consideration. Stated another way, we may say that each of the laws, even the seemingly insignificant ones, is an attempt to exposit and apply the first commandment:[11] "You shall have no other gods before me." "Laws," or better *Toroth,* are attempts to affirm the sovereignty of God over every aspect of life. This Torah is compelling and inclusive precisely because of the exclusiveness and intolerance of this God. He wills all of life to serve him and him alone (see Deut. 6:4-9). In contrast to law elsewhere in the ancient Near East, this legal material is *theological* in a decisive way.

The law collections have various thrusts in getting at this single purpose. The Covenant Code (Exod. 21:1—23:19) is a relatively early collection which has little distinctively Israelite character beyond the claim of Yahweh's sovereignty. The Holiness Code (Lev. 18-26) has as its thesis that God is holy and that if Israel would live in relation to him, then she also must be holy. She must be distinctive and operate for different reasons from the rest of society. The priestly collections are concerned with the sin of Israel and in very specific ways describe how this God who is so awful in his holiness can meet with this people in its impurity and unworthiness. The answer is given through an elaborate cultic apparatus which safeguards the holiness of God while permitting his presence in the midst of his people.

Though not so explicit in P as in the others, there is a shared conviction that Israel must not be as the Canaanites. She must not accept the ways of the world, for she is called to serve a different God and her life must reflect this. Thus the laws function to define what it means to be God's people. They explore how to live with this God. They also illuminate Israel's involvements in the pressures of history and the temptations to syncretism which are always present. They insist that the life of faith must be kept free from significant perversion.

When we come to consider the prophets in detail, we will want to study the ways in which the prophets look back to these legal traditions. The primary concern of these prophets is to indict Israel for not honoring the covenant relation. On numerous occasions, this indictment is grounded in specific "laws" which have been violated. The judgment which the prophets pronounce upon Israel is characteristically not vague and general. It is most often precise and names specific offenses. The prophets repeatedly utilize the old legal traditions to determine the present status of Israel.

The Covenant Traditions of History and Law in the Cult

Clearly, we do not have detached historical traditions which are simply a tribute to the past, or legal traditions which are memories from an archaic system of social order. Rather in the tradition of Israel we have a dynamic and continuing interaction of historical and legal traditions with new situations. The historical traditions bear witness to the graciousness of Yahweh toward Israel, and the legal traditions manifest Yahweh's claim upon Israel. It is this healthy and dynamic interrelation between historical and legal tradition, between God's graciousness and his claim, which is at the center of Israel's faith in every new circumstance. The delicate relation of God's graciousness and God's claim is most problematic for the community of faith. Without the first, the community becomes paralyzed in moralism and legalism and prophetic ministry is expressed as scolding people for not being good. Without the second, the community becomes complacent and undisciplined and prophetic ministry is expressed as comforting the comfortable.

When we talk about the interaction of the tradition with the new situation, we obviously are not speaking about written sources, for written sources cannot interact. Rather, we refer to the community, which utilized the sources in its public worship. The covenant faith of Israel which has its center in the meeting of these two (tradition, new situation) was maintained, repeatedly renewed, and revitalized in the great festivals of public worship. Though the precise details of these events are perhaps beyond recovery, it is now generally agreed that the cultic assemblies had as their concern the covenant relation, and what was said and done centered in that relation. In chapter IV the meaning of "cult" will be explored more fully. By the term I mean the official public acts of worship in Israel. The cult is not simply a shadow of the real covenant life of Israel, as Westermann seems to suggest. On the other hand it does not encompass every important aspect of Israel's existence, as Mowinckel suggests. Though we lack a scholarly consensus on the precise character of Israel's cult, it is clear that her worship had to do with the great themes of covenant. Canaanite influences and perversions were no doubt present. But the distinctive elements in Israel's public worship concern covenant history and covenant responsibility. Differences of opinion among scholars involve the question of Israel's borrowing from her neighbors and Israel's resistance to the pressures of her neighbors. Obviously she both borrowed and resisted. The data is summarized in H. J. Kraus, *Worship in Israel*.[12]

The liturgy of this worship, then, is covenant liturgy. It may have served varied purposes, depending upon the status of the covenant relation. When the covenant relation was in good repair, worship may have been primarily a joyful and grateful remembering. But more often, public worship was intended to (a) lead Israel to new appreciation of the covenant which had *fallen into disuse* or (b) to lead to renewal of covenant which had been *disrupted by infidelity* on the part of Israel.

It is this latter situation which concerns us, i.e., these events in the worship life of Israel when covenant was renewed or restored. The current understanding of this worship is supported primarily by the parallels which have been discovered in the political treaties and alliances known in ancient political documents.[13] As in most formal relationships, the procedure was fixed and not free, so that the steps taken follow a regular pattern:

  (a) The naming of the great king, the one who grants the treaty to the lesser party, including titles and attributes which do honor to him.

  (b) The recitation of past deeds of graciousness by the king directed toward the lesser party.

  (c) The covenant stipulations in which the greater member of the treaty gives the conditions upon which the relation will exist, i.e., the obligations imposed upon the lesser member.

  (d) The oath of loyalty by the lesser member which includes an acceptance of the conditions just pronounced.

  (e) A recital of the blessings and curses which will result from honoring or dishonoring the treaty.

Thus we have a fixed form by which formal relations were established, with guarantees to maintain the relationship.

Though the exact relation is far from clear, an analysis of the structure of the covenant liturgy of Israel demonstrates very close parallels in procedure:

  (a) The naming of the great king:

> I am the LORD your God, who brought you out of the land of Egypt, out of the house of bondage (Exod. 20:2).

> Thus says the LORD, the God of Israel (Joshua 24:2).

  (b) Recitation of past deeds of graciousness:

> You have seen what I did to the Egyptians, and how I bore you on eagles' wings and brought you to myself (Exod. 19:4; cf. 20:2b).

> The long recital of Joshua 24: 2b-13.

  (c) The covenant stipulations:

> You shall have no other gods before me (Exod. 20:3). Cf. the complete decalogue, vss. 3-17, and the Covenant Code which follows, Exod. 21:1—23:19.

> Now therefore fear the LORD, and serve him in sincerity and in faithfulness; put away the gods . . . (24:14-15; cf. vs. 25).

(d) The oath of obedience:

All the words which the LORD has spoken we will do (Exod. 24:3).	Far be it from us that we should forsake the LORD, to serve other gods (24:16).
	Nay; but we will serve the LORD (24:21).
	The LORD our God we will serve, and his voice we will obey (24:24).

(e) A recital of the blessings and curses:

. . . I will bless your bread and your water; and I will take sickness away from the midst of you (Exod. 23:25).	If you forsake the LORD and serve foreign gods, then he will turn and do you harm, and consume you . . . (24:20).

To be sure, the form is not in every point precisely parallel and in each sequence some elements are lacking. However, we are not concerned with an exact analysis but with the general structure. It is this structure which is fundamental to an understanding of the prophets. The prophets speak to a people which is more or less familiar with this view of life, which knows that she owes her existence to the graciousness of Yahweh. This view of life is expressed in Israel's use of a political idiom for her faith, namely, the language of treaty covenant. For whatever reason, Israel rejected the religious idiom of her neighbors which attempted to hold the cosmos together and manipulate the gods. Instead, Israel knew that her role in history is not to manipulate but to obey. She saw that meaning is not found in the wholeness of the cosmos but in the brokenness of history. She affirmed that the human community is not a spectator to the actions of the gods but is caught up in those actions and is forced to decide. She learned that the goal of life is not escape from problems but involvement in the building of a just community. All this is implicit in the use of a "political" rather than a "religious" idiom.[14]

The prophets then attempt to work out in various historical situations the implications of the covenant liturgy for the life and destiny of Israel. When we say in what follows that the prophets are integrally linked to the old traditions, it is in the framework of this covenant structure that we speak. This structure in its various forms is at the heart of the worship, life, and self-understanding of Israel. The prophets attempt to say to Israel that the graciousness and the claim of God known in the covenant liturgy must be her primary concern even in "today's" kind of world.

The central concern of the prophets was to communicate to Israel what it meant to be Israel. Or to say it in contemporary language, they were concerned with the nature and the mission of the church. The covenant liturgy had made it clear that Israel's primary *loyalty* was to this gracious God who had confronted her in her moments of despair and need. Concerning her *purpose* in life, Israel had vowed to give herself to Yahweh through the keeping of the covenant commandments. But in working out her loyalty and her purpose, Israel had turned away from the focus of covenant, which meant she had denied the very foundations of her existence. It is to this dishonoring of covenant that the prophets address themselves. It is an urgent concern, for related to it is the question of Israel's historical survival.

II.

The Prophets and the Traditions of Covenant

In the next three chapters we will consider various aspects of the relation of the prophets to the old covenant traditions. In the present chapter we will consider the ways in which the prophets employed the actual *content of the old traditions* to address their contemporaries. We shall seek to show that the prophets did not ground their message in novel ideals of their own, but that they can be understood only in terms of their frequent appeal to the memories of the tradition. Their concern in using these traditions is to explore the relevance of the traditions for the present circumstance of the covenant people. The prophetic use of these traditions transforms them so that they are not simply recollections of past events. The traditions now serve to add urgency and a radical dimension by which the appeal of faith in the present moment is made more compelling.

The Historical Traditions

The great deeds of God which Israel remembered from the distant past are reaffirmed by the prophets. The prophets use the tradition of great deeds not only to testify to the graciousness of Yahweh but to contrast his continuing deeds of goodness with the present infidelity and ingratitude of Israel. The prophets give the tradition a fresh role. The tradition serves to expose Israel's response to Yahweh as ineffective and superficial. The memory of Yahweh's goodness in the past supports the charge of infidelity made against Israel.

1. THE EXODUS TRADITION

This central tradition of Israel's memory is at the center of Hosea's proclamation to Israel. Several allusions to "return to Egypt" imply that Israel came into existence only by gracious deliverance from Egypt (Hosea 8:13; 9:3; 11:5). Thus the prophet speaks about the "undoing of Israel." Characteristically, the Exodus motif stands at the beginning of a new pericope. Hosea begins at Israel's beginning. Israel hears what he has to say in the present time only in the context of this great event at the beginning of Israel's history:

> When Israel was a child, I loved him,
>   and out of Egypt I called my son (11:1).

This is both a general allusion to the Exodus and a more specific reference to Exodus 4:22:

> Thus says the LORD, Israel is my first-born son, and I say to you,
> "Let my son go that he may serve me."

The utter graciousness of that event is stressed by Hosea. It concerns love for a helpless and insignificant child. So great is his love!

So also in Hosea 13:4 the reference stands at the beginning:

> I am the LORD your God
>   from the land of Egypt;
> you know no God but me,
>   and besides me, there is no savior.

Both of these references to the Exodus affirm that it was only by sheer grace that Israel was brought out. Israel has historical identity only because Yahweh acted in his great love.

These two affirmations stand at the beginning of parallel units. In both cases the next verses function as contrasts to describe Israel's stubborn response:

> The more I called them,
>   the more they went from me;
> they kept sacrificing to the Baals,
>   and burning incense to idols.
>   ... they did not know that I healed them (11:2, 3b).

> but when they had fed to the full,
>> they were filled, and their heart was lifted up;
>> therefore they forgot me (13:6).

After the contrast between the past graciousness of Yahweh in the Exodus and Israel's unfaithful response, both units draw a conclusion for the present. Destruction will come:

> They shall return to the land of Egypt,
>> and Assyria shall be their king,
>> because they have refused to return to me.
> The sword shall rage against their cities,
>> consume the bars of their gates,
>> and devour them in their fortresses (11:5-6).

> So I will be to them like a lion,
>> like a leopard I will lurk beside the way.
>>> . . . . .
> and there I will devour them like a lion,
>> as a wild beast would rend them (13:7-8).

Judgment upon Israel and the promise of destruction is possible only in the context of the old tradition. The prophet begins with the Exodus event to give power and urgency to the judgment he must pronounce. The words the prophet must speak can be felt and understood only by those who have appropriated the memory as their own.

A similar use of the memory is found in 12:7-14, but the sequence is reversed. There the unit begins with the indictment about false weights and oppression in verses 7-8. Then the historical memory is invoked in verse 9:

> I am the LORD your God
>> from the land of Egypt.

The threat follows in verse 9b. Between the indictment and the punishment the historical reference gives focus to the entire proclamation.

In the very difficult unit of 12:10-13, verse 13 also alludes to the Exodus:

> By a prophet the LORD brought Israel up from Egypt,
>> and by a prophet he was preserved.

Here again, the reference to Exodus emphasizes the fact that Israel has not responded to the concern and attention Yahweh has given her (vs. 14). The prophet recalls this great saving deed so that Israel may be more fully aware of her failure and the devastation she has brought upon herself.

2. THE PATRIARCHAL TRADITION

In general the prophets do not employ the patriarchal tradition until the exilic period. Presumably this is because they do not wish to emphasize the tradition about the free promise of God. They prefer to stress the Exodus tradition and the conditional character of covenant.[1] Nevertheless, Hosea does refer to the promise tradition of the patriarchs.

In the extraordinary passage of 11:8-9 he refers to it only to depart from it:

> How can I give you up, O Ephraim!
> How can I hand you over, O Israel!
> How can I make you like Admah!
> How can I treat you like Zeboiim!
> My heart recoils within me . . .

The first two lines are simply an address to the people of Israel under two names. But the references to Admah and Zeboiim refer back to Sodom and Gomorrah (Gen. 18-19; cf. Gen. 10:19; 14:2, 8; Deut. 29:23) which were destroyed because of their wickedness, "Because the outcry against Sodom and Gomorrah is great and their sin is very grave" (Gen. 18:20). In contrast to them, Abraham and his house are to do "righteousness" and "justice" (Gen. 18:19). Those who do not live in this relation of covenant responsibility must be destroyed. Hence Sodom and Gomorrah are "overthrown" (Gen. 19:25).

In this context the word usage of Hosea is noteworthy. We may now understand why Hosea employs this reference. He makes a critique of the traditional understanding of Yahweh's action toward those who do not honor covenant in order to emphasize his own radical affirmation. There must indeed be "overthrowing" but no longer will it be of the disobedient cities. Now the "overthrowing" is in the heart of Yahweh. It is not accidental that the prophet employs precisely the same word as does the old covenant tradition. In Genesis 19:25 the RSV rendering is "overthrew," and in Hosea 11:8 the same term is rendered "recoil." But to set the word in Hosea in the context of the Sodom-Gomorrah tradition alters the meaning decisively. In the old tradition, upheaval caused the destruction of the cities. In the prophetic handling of the tradition, the upheaval has been internalized by Yahweh, so great is his fidelity toward Israel.

The use of the old tradition and even the old word in this critical way permits Hosea to make an affirmation about the graciousness of Yahweh after the indictment and threat of verses 1-7. In contrast to Genesis 18-19, Yahweh here deals with broken covenant by the agony (overthrowing) of forgiveness. Again, Hosea's affirmation is a very vigorous one because it stands in relation to the sacral tradition about a God who distinguishes between the faithful and the unfaithful. Hosea not only inverts the meaning of the old tradition but he also departs from the view of his contemporaries (Isaiah 1:9-10; Amos 4:11, which also uses the same verb, "overthrow"), who employ the tradition for more conventional purposes. Hosea 11:8-9 is an excellent example of a creative use of a historical tradition to affirm the very antithesis of its original intention.[2]

The other clear allusion in Hosea to the tradition of the fathers is in 12:2-6. There the play on the name Jacob employs the characteristic identification of the Northern Kingdom and the patriarch of the same name. The unit combines several traditional references to serve a quite new purpose. The clan saga of Genesis 25:23-26 which affirms the superiority of Israel to Edom is recalled in verse 3:

> In the womb he took his brother by the heel . . .

This is followed by the cult legend of Penuel (Gen. 32:22-32):

> . . . in his manhood he strove with God.
> He strove with the angel and prevailed,
>   he wept and sought his favor (vss. 3b-4a),

and the unit is concluded with the name taken from another cult legend (Gen. 28:10-22):

He met God at Bethel,
  and there God spoke with him (vs. 4b).

The original stories extol the people Israel and celebrate the authenticity of the two shrines mentioned. But Hosea uses them for the sake of his own message, namely, to indict Israel for her infidelity (vs. 2), and to call her to return to the covenant. This call, which contains the fundamental words of covenant, is stated in a three-member imperative:

"So you by the help of your God, *return,*
  hold fast to love and justice,
  and *wait* continually for your God" (vs. 6).

We may appreciate the use of the old tradition from two perspectives. First, the present use introduces into it very strong covenantal dimensions which were not so explicit in its earlier context. Second, the appeal of the prophet indicts Israel not only for present guilt but also for the burden of an entire history of unfaithfulness to covenant, even when Yahweh has been gracious. Israel has disobeyed the one who sustained father Jacob. The present guilt is an inseparable part of a long history of infidelity. The tradition underscores the condition of covenant and the urgent need for complete repentance.

The use of the Abraham (Hosea 11:8-9) and now the Jacob tradition is suggestive. Hosea uses Abraham material for an extraordinary affirmation about the graciousness of Yahweh which transcends the original tradition. He uses the Jacob tradition for a penetrating indictment of Israel in her guilt in the context of Yahweh's act of grace.[3] He employs both traditions to deepen his radical proclamation of covenant.

3. THE SOJOURN TRADITION

Hosea utilizes the sojourn motif extensively in a variety of ways. From it he derives some of his basic images. One of the primary uses is that of 5:1-2.

For the judgment pertains to you;
  for you have been a snare at Mizpah,
  and a net spread upon Tabor.

> And they have made deep the pit of Shittim;
>   but I will chastise all of them.

It is the reference to Shittim which concerns us, for this is apparently an allusion to Baal-Peor:

> While Israel dwelt in Shittim the people began to play the harlot with the daughters of Moab. These invited the people to the sacrifices of their gods, and the people ate, and bowed down to their gods. So Israel yoked himself to Baal of Peor (Num. 25:1-3).

This historical allusion has become a type for Hosea. It contains the basic notion of *harlotry* of which Hosea makes so much (see especially chapter 4).

In the context of this historical allusion, Hosea views the entire history of Israel under the image of marriage. He sees the basic thrust of Israel's existence as covenant breaking in the form of harlotry. Hosea views every aspect of life, especially cult and foreign policy, as a form of harlotry. He describes the financial profit from political involvement as "gifts from lovers" (2:12). Present infidelity which we take for granted is as repulsive to Yahweh as the abhorrent act of Numbers 25:1-4. It is now irrelevant to say, "We wouldn't do anything like that." Hosea employs the old tradition as a general statement about the rottenness and decadence of Israel's syncretism.[4]

The Baal-Peor tradition recurs in 9:10 together with a quite different sojourn allusion:

> Like grapes in the wilderness,
>   I found Israel.
> Like the first fruit on the fig tree,
>   in its first season,
>   I saw your fathers.
> But they came to Baal-peor,
>   and consecrated themselves to Baal,
>   and became detestable like the thing they loved.

The latter half of the verse is a reassertion of the same abhorrence we have found in 5:1-2. But the first half looks at the sojourn from a quite different point of view. Here the basic idea is one of gracious election. Israel was at that point young, alive, wild, and Yahweh entered into a meaningful relation with great expectation for future productivity.

The image potently combines the two ideas: (a) that Yahweh acted in graciousness in choosing Israel for his own (Deut. 32:10-14), and (b) that Israel acted unfaithfully and ungraciously in turning from the one in the wilderness to the Baal of Peor. Utilizing this combination, 9:11-14 continues to make the threat on the basis of the indictment. Again, the present community is to bear the guilt of the entire history of Israel, the long history from election until now, all of which is a history of disobedience. The interaction of past and present makes the direct action of Yahweh in contemporary history all the more awesome and forbidding.

In chapter 11, the wilderness motif follows immediately upon the Exodus motif which we have already considered:

> Yet it was I who taught Ephraim to walk,
> > I took them up in my arms;
> > but they did not know that I healed them (vs. 3).

Again, the prophet makes reference to the early period of the young child Israel when the father (cf. Exod. 4:22) nurtures and trains him. This presumably is the period between the Exodus (birth) and entrance into the land (maturity). More specifically the reference to healer may recall Exodus 15:26b: ". . . for [surely] I am the LORD, your healer."

The climactic affirmation of Hosea 11:3 comes after a discussion of the Exodus event (vs. 1). Thus Hosea employs the old tradition to show that the recent history of Israel has been a denial of the tradition. In the older narrative Yahweh is known as healer. According to Hosea, contemporary Israel has completely forgotten this dimension of her history. The positive affirmation of the tradition serves to intensify the present indictment, again by means of contrast (cf. Jer. 8:22).

The next allusion to the sojourn motif is in 12:9b. It follows the Exodus motif already discussed:

> I will again make you dwell in tents,
> > as in the days of the appointed feast.

Because of the indictment of verses 7-8, Israel will return to the situation of the wilderness period. The context suggests that this is meant to be punishment. By her disobedience, Israel has forfeited her life in the land. But elsewhere (2:14), Hosea regards the desert as the place of renewal and restored covenant. It may be that the motifs of both punishment and renewal are present here. The punishment is chastisement and purgation which will lead to right relation. But the circumstance which leads to the renewed covenant is one of hardship and complete dependence. Israel is aware that she cannot survive without Yahweh. Hosea has correctly understood the main thrust of the sojourn tradition[5] and has taken the dependence motif and made it the center of his new affirmation. Stripped of all other supports, Israel will learn again that her life is intimately bound up in covenant. To turn from the covenant Lord is the way to death (cf. Deut. 30:15-20).

In a usage very much like 11:3, 13:5 employs the wilderness motif to ramify the Exodus event of the preceding verse:

> It was I who knew you in the wilderness,
>   in the land of drought.

Here the positive side of the tradition is stressed. Israel survived in the wilderness only by the continuing sustenance of Yahweh. Repeatedly there was desperation for water (Exod. 15:22-25; 17:6; Num. 20:10-11), and a protest against Yahweh and the Moses-Aaron leadership motivated by a fear of death. But each time Yahweh's power gave life-giving water to save and enliven. Again, Hosea affirms that Israel's life is utterly dependent upon Yahweh. He can be trusted to do good for his people.

This allusion supports the gracious affirmation of 13:4 and leads abruptly and inevitably to the harsh indictment of verse 6:

> but when they had fed to the full,
>   they were filled, and their heart was lifted up;
>   therefore they forgot me (cf. Deut. 32:15-18).

The use of the tradition in verse 5 gives the indictment its sharp bite and prepares the way for the threat of verses 7-8. Death comes to those who reject the graciousness revealed in the old traditions.

Two basic points are made by the use of this tradition. (a) Israel has been treated with utter graciousness and will live as she accepts this mode of existence. (b) Israel has acted in profound rejection of this relation through her many modes of harlotry. In both dimensions, the radicalness of Hosea's indictment is reinforced by the memory of sojourn.

4. PRE-MONARCHAL HISTORY IN THE LAND

Though it cannot be counted as a major motif of the early traditions of Israel, we must note the considerable use Hosea makes of the historical memory of that period in Israel's life after the entrance into the land and before the establishment of the monarchy, roughly 1250-1000 B.C. This was the period during which Israel became settled in the land and to some extent stabilized. Though he never considers it in detail, Hosea regards this period as one of syncretism when Israel accommodated herself to the culture and religion of Canaan.[6] For that reason Hosea asserts that restored covenant is possible only by a return to the wilderness. This is necessary if Israel is to be free from cultural pressures and temptations. To identify with Canaanite culture, to compromise the radical faith which he attributes to the wilderness period, is to alter the foundations of the community and thereby cease to be Israel. Hosea, along with the Northern traditions of Deuteronomy and Jeremiah, is primarily concerned with what it means to be Israel. He makes frequent allusions to this period of history to heap up evidence for the indictment that Israel has really ceased to be Israel; i.e., she has failed to understand her existence and destiny in relation to the covenant God:

> Israel has forgotten his Maker (8:14).

The indictment is rooted in past deeds:

> They have deeply corrupted themselves
>   as in the days of Gibe-ah:
> he will remember their iniquity,
>   he will punish their sins (9:9).

> Every evil of theirs is in Gilgal;
>   there I began to hate them (9:15a).

> From the days of Gibe-ah, you have sinned, O Israel;
>   there they have continued.
> Shall not war overtake them in Gibe-ah? (10:9).

> If there is iniquity in Gilead
>   they shall surely come to nought;
> if in Gilgal they sacrifice bulls,
>   their altars also shall be like stone heaps
>   on the furrows of the field (12:11).

These are not mere polemics against cultic activities but constitute a much deeper indictment. The allusions to Gibeah may refer to the sordid narrative of Judges 19-20 in which the men of Gibeah violated the structure and community of Israel:

> "What wickedness is this that has taken place among you? Now therefore give up the men, the base fellows in Gibe-ah, that we may put them to death, and *put away evil from Israel.*" But the Benjaminites would not listen to the voice of their brethren, *the people of Israel* (Judges 20:12-13).

Clearly the offense here is not a moral defect but failure to take seriously the nature of Israel as a covenant community.[7] By alluding to this narrative the prophet reminds Israel that the basic act of disobedience is in misunderstanding what it means to be God's covenant people.[8]

The other possible allusion in the Gibeah reference may be the whole Saul episode (see 1 Sam. 10), in which the kingship of Saul begins the rejection of the charismatic ordering of the community. Even though Saul is far removed from the developments under Solomon, he begins the movement to alter radically the foundations of community life.[9] The political efforts of Saul, at least to the orthodox, constitute an act of unfaith, a refusal to rely upon the God of the old traditions (I Sam. 13, 15). Either or both of the possible Gibeah references bespeak an indictment for refusing to be a covenant community; i.e., for coming to terms with Canaanite understandings of life in cult and in politics.[10]

The Gilgal references constitute the same indictment. It may be a reference to Canaanite syncretism in cultic activity (1 Sam. 10:8; 11:15; 13:8-10; 15:21; cf. Amos 4:4; 5:5; Micah 6:5) or a reference to the innovation of kingship (1 Sam. 11:15). In either case, Hosea shows that the present problems of the covenant community have deep roots which betray the true character of Israel. The present community can only understand its dilemma in the context of these historical traditions.

The Legal Traditions in Hosea

Our discussion of the use of legal traditions by Hosea will summarize the numerous allusions to the old laws in this tradition. Use of old legal tradition shows that the prophet does not condemn Israel only generally or arbitrarily, but very specifically according to known conditions of covenant.[11] The indictment[12] concerns the violation of specific covenant stipulations accepted by Israel in solemn covenant making. Presumably she heard and accepted these stipulations repeatedly in the liturgy of covenant renewal.

Before beginning our analysis of the specific regulations, we may pause briefly to note that the prophet also makes sweeping statements declaring that the covenant and covenant law have been violated:

> because you have rejected knowledge,
> I reject you from being a priest to me.
> And since you have forgotten *the law* of your God,
> I also will forget your children (4:6).

> But at Adam they transgressed the *covenant*;
> there they dealt treacherously with me (6:7).

> Woe to them, for they have strayed from me!
> Destruction to them, for they have *rebelled against me*! (7:13),

> because they have broken my covenant,
> and transgressed *my law* (8:1).

> Were I to write for him *my laws* by ten thousands,
> they would be regarded as a strange thing (8:12).

> . . . Israel has forgotten his Maker (8:14).

This last reference is not as explicit, but it certainly makes an allusion to the great events by which Israel came into being (Exodus as creation event).

> They utter mere words;
> with empty oaths they make covenants (10:4).

Here the reference is to other covenants and alliances which violate the exclusiveness of the covenant with Yahweh (cf. 12:1). In a variety of ways, some by direct mention of covenant and Torah, others by indirection, Hosea speaks judgment against Israel be-

cause the conditions of covenant have been violated. Much of the
tradition of Hosea is a bill of particulars upon this charge. One
cannot understand or accept this indictment unless it is seen in the
context of covenant law.

1. THE DECALOGUE

Though the setting and the date of the decalogue are uncertain,
it is clear that the decalogue was fixed and known by the time of
Hosea. He bases much of his indictment upon it. Before looking
at specifics, we may note that 4:2 is the programmatic statement
for what follows. It is a summary of the decalogue:

> There is no faithfulness or kindness,
>   and no knowledge of God in the land;
> there is swearing (cf. Exod. 20:7),
>   lying (cf. Exod. 20:16),
>   killing (cf. Exod. 20:13),
>   stealing (cf. Exod. 20:15), and
>   committing adultery (cf. Exod. 20:14);
> they break all bounds and murder follows murder.

The basic statement of the sin of Israel is a clear reference to the
ten commandments (see Jer. 7:9 for a like statement).

The first commandment, "You shall have no other gods before
me," obviously is a general statement to which any indictment
may refer. But some statements by the prophet seem particularly
closely related:

> . . . they have strayed from me!
>   . . . they have rebelled against me! (7:13).

> They turn to Baal;
>   they are like a treacherous bow (7:16).

> The more I called them,
>   the more they went from me;
> they kept sacrificing to the Baals,
>   and burning incense to idols (11:2).

> My people are bent on turning away from me (11:7).

With the polemic against syncretism, Hosea employs the substance
of the first commandment to condemn Israel for moving the center

of life away from Yahweh to other seemingly more attractive options (see 5:3-4; 8:14; 9:10; 10:4), in terms of both cult and political relations. Israel, by entering into the world of Canaanite religion and power politics, has forgotten the covenantal basis of life. She has denied her exclusive relation with this jealous God.

The indictment for making images follows the second command: "You shall not make for yourself a graven image" (Exod. 20:4; cf. Exod. 20:23; Lev. 19:4; Exod. 34:17). This offense also derives from involvement in the non-covenantal values of Canaan.

> My people inquire of a thing of wood,
>   and their staff gives them oracles (4:12a).

> With their silver and gold they made idols
>   for their own destruction.
>   . . . . .
> A workman made it;
>   it is not God (8:4b-5b).

> and [they] make for themselves molten images,
> idols skilfully made of their silver,
>   all of them the work of craftsmen.
> Sacrifice to these, they say.
> Men kiss calves! (13:2).

To be sure, this concerns more than mere images. As the commandment suggests, this is a basic denial of the free sovereign character of God, which Israel has forgotten (cf. 4:17; 10:5; 11:2).[13] When Israel forgets who Yahweh is, she also forgets that her own existence is bound in covenant with him.

The third command is: "You shall not take the name of the LORD your God in vain" (Exod. 20:7). At least once this is alluded to:

> They utter mere words;
>   with empty oaths they make covenants (10:4).

The term rendered "empty" is the same word as in the prohibition of Exodus 20:7. Though the indictment is not explicitly linked to Yahweh, certainly it refers to light and perverse oaths based on the name and guarantee of Yahweh. This means the exploitation rather than service of Yahweh, for purposes not in keeping with

his will for covenant. The deity has been reduced to a guarantor
of "our plans" and is no longer lord of the community.

The fourth commandment concerns the holiness of the Sabbath
day (Exod. 20:8). Though there is no direct use of it, there is a
suggestion that punishment will put an end to the great days of
festal joy:

> And I will put an end to all her mirth,
>> her feasts, her new moons, her sabbaths,
>> and all her appointed feasts (2:11).

Obviously, if it is stopped, then it can no longer be "kept" or
"observed" (Deut. 5:12). The ending of the Sabbath is more than
the cessation of a holiday. Because the day is in the context of
Exodus (Deut. 5:15) its cessation becomes a denial of Exodus
and so an undoing of Israel. What is taken from Israel in this
sentence is the whole ordering by which she understood herself.
Thus the commandment is turned to be a most drastic threat.

Though the indictment which precedes the threat does not say
the Sabbath has been profaned, there is a general denunciation
which suggests that all of life has been polluted. One is left to
assume that these cultic occasions have also been violated. Moving
one step away from the Sabbath to the general worship life of the
community, Hosea declares:

> Rejoice not, O Israel!
>> Exult not like the peoples;
> for you have played the harlot, forsaking your God.
>> You have loved a harlot's hire
>> upon all threshing floors (9:1).

The mention of threshing floors refers to fertility worship.[14] Moreover, the warning not to rejoice "like the peoples" is an accusation
that Israel's worship has been contaminated by the mood, intention, and practice of the Canaanite cult (see 1 Sam. 8:5, 20). The
specific violation is a manifestation of the fundamental infidelity
of Israel.

The next commandment, which concerns honoring parents
(Exod. 20:12), deals with a domestic relation which we would
not expect Hosea to comment upon. Yet he uses the image of
parenthood to further indict Israel:

When Israel was a child, I loved him,
and out of Egypt I called my son.
The more I called them,
the more they went from me;

. . . . .

Yet it was I who taught Ephraim to walk,
I took them up in my arms;
but they did not know that I healed them (11:1-3).

This father has done far more than a father need do for a son.
Yet in response, the son has not honored his father. He has gone
away and has entered into other relations. To be sure, the commandment is given a theological turn, but the indictment of this
chapter could not be understood apart from this law (cf. Deut.
21:18-21; Isa. 1:2).

The prophet refers to the sixth commandment (Exod. 20:13)
only once, again with a deepened notion of guilt:

Gilead is a city of evildoers,
tracked with blood.
As robbers lie in wait for a man,
so the priests are banded together;
they murder[15] on the way to Shechem,
yea, they commit villainy (6:8-9).

This, in addition to being an indictment for murder, is a judgment
upon the priestly leadership of the community.[16] All stand guilty,
because they have killed, even though the law said, "You shall not
kill" (cf. 12:14).

It is with the seventh commandment concerning adultery that
we see the fullest use made of the law by Hosea. Though the term
of Exodus 20:14 occurs only six times, the figure of harlotry and
fickleness is much more widely used. Here we confine ourselves to
the use of the term from the decalogue:

Therefore your daughters play the harlot,
and your brides *commit adultery.*
I will not punish your daughters when they play the harlot,
nor your brides when they *commit adultery*;
for the men themselves go aside with harlots,
and sacrifice with cult prostitutes,
and a people without understanding shall come to ruin (4:13-14).

> They are all *adulterers*;
>   they are like a heated oven,
> whose baker ceases to stir the fire,
>   from the kneading of the dough until it is leavened (7:4).

These two uses are representative of the motif in Hosea. The first takes the image literally, and refers to cultic prostitution. But the second reference expands the image so that adultery refers no longer to a sexual act only, but to corruption and wicked deeds (7:1), treachery and intrigue (vss. 3, 6), and the general conduct of foreign policy (vs. 7). This figure, as the others, is used to describe the wholesale degeneration of the covenant community. One important aspect of this was sacral prostitution according to Canaanite rites. But it extended into every sphere of life.

Hosea uses the term "steal" found in Exodus 20:15 only once:

> for they deal falsely,
>   the thief breaks in,
>   and the bandits raid without (7:1b).

The context indicates that Hosea is not speaking simply of acts of thievery; cultic and political acts and governmental policies may also be described in these terms. The statement of 7:1a indicates how seriously these offenses are taken. Such behavior blocks the healing purposes of Yahweh.

The prohibition on bearing false witness is not referred to directly, but again the allusion gives the law a theological stress:

> I would redeem them,
>   but they speak lies against me (7:13b).

The real offense of Israel in false witness is not in social community relations but in their refusal or inability to live faithfully with this God. In this passage, judicial language is employed. In relation to Yahweh, Israel is like a lying witness on the stand.[17] In another legal formulation in Leviticus 19:11 the same warnings, very similar to the decalogue, are recited. There the warning on false-hood uses a word which does not occur in the decalogue. Hosea applies this term (4:2; 7:1; 10:13; 12:1) not just to "lies" but to the whole basis of covenant life. Thus in 10:13 the term is parallel to "iniquity" and "injustice." Again, the simple prohibition of the decalogue is deepened and broadened to encompass the whole life of Israel. Israel has more than false vows. Her whole life of deception and falseness is judged by this commandment.

It is striking that the tenth commandment, on coveting, is absent in this tradition which so emphasizes the images of inordinate desire.

This summary of evidence scarcely needs comment. Hosea has employed the formulations of the decalogue to show that in every dimension of life, in every conceivable way, Israel has dishonored the covenant relation. She has compromised the exclusiveness of covenant. She has syncretized with non-Israelite views of life and worship, and has been fickle toward her covenant God. Though Hosea has employed the decalogue, his restatement does not simply charge violation of the laws. Through imaginative handling, he has converted the prohibitions into a profound theological critique of the character and quality of Israel's existence. The covenant people are understood in terms of their response to the covenant law. Hosea is precise and firm in showing that Israel has failed in her response.

2. DEUTERONOMY

Many scholars have noted the particularly close affinities between Hosea and Deuteronomy.[18] Many of the same concerns which reflected the decalogue are also reflected in Deuteronomy, and we need not review each of these. But there are other concerns which betray close affinities to Deuteronomy which should be noted. I do not refer to literary dependence but rather to the appropriation of a living tradition which received its literary expression in Deuteronomy. This relation is important for understanding the context out of which the proclamation of Hosea emerged. It links Hosea to the Northern tradition of amphictyony. We do not have a man copying a document but a member of the community drawing perceptively and creatively upon the traditions of the community.

(1) General Concerns Related to Deuteronomy

Several motifs pervasive in Hosea have rootage in Deuteronomy. Primary among these is the *fear of foreigners* and relations with them:

". . . then you must utterly destroy them; you shall make no covenant with them, and show no mercy to them. You shall not make marriages with them, giving your daughters to their sons or taking their daughters for your sons. For they would turn away your sons from following me, to serve other gods; then the anger of the LORD would be kindled against you, and he would destroy you quickly" (Deut. 7:2b-4).

Deuteronomy is not primarily concerned with external ideas of purity, but is aware of the dangers of syncretism and the temptation to compromise the intolerance of covenant with the jealous God.[19]

This motif is recurrent in Hosea:

> They have dealt faithlessly with the LORD;
> for they have borne alien children (5:7a).

> Aliens devour his strength,
> and he knows it not (7:9a).

> The standing grain has no heads,
> it shall yield no meal;
> if it were to yield,
> aliens would devour it.
> Israel is swallowed up;
> already they are among the nations
> as a useless vessel.
> For they have gone up to Assyria,
> a wild ass wandering alone;
> Ephraim has hired lovers (8:7b-9; cf. 5:13; 12:1).

What had been a warning against intermarriage in Deuteronomy is, in Hosea, a polemic against all intercourse with foreigners, whether political, commercial, or military. Faithfulness to the covenant means to be free from all other involvements and loyalties. Again a very specific admonition appears now as a general affirmation of the meaning of covenant faithfulness.

The central theological issue of *covenant faithfulness* is also developed in terms of Deuteronomic ideas. The statement of Hosea 4:11 is that wine and new wine take away "the heart of my people," the heart being the center of loyalty and decision-making.[20] They are unable to choose or honor the choices they have made. This is an indictment which is closely related to the summons of Deuteronomy 6:5: "You shall love the LORD your God with all *your heart.*" The intolerance of Yahweh toward his people is compromised by Israel's participation in Canaanite ritual which ignores his claim.

Of course Deuteronomy expressed the epitome of covenant faithfulness in 6:4:

> *Hear*, O Israel, Yahweh is your God, Yahweh only.

This summons receives an echo in Hosea 9:17:

> My God will cast them off,
>   because they did not *hear* him,
>   they shall be wanderers among the nations.

The use of "hear" ("hearken") is most likely a reference to Deuteronomy 6:4. The prophet condemns Israel on the basis of a very clear and most prominent command. By not listening, Israel has rejected the core of the covenant.[21]

The sermons of Deuteronomy 6 and 8 repeatedly stress the importance of Israel's remembering the graciousness of Yahweh and Israel's dependence upon him. There is danger in forgetting (Deuteronomy 6:12, 15). Israel is tempted to think that human ingenuity produced the blessings which she now enjoys (Deut. 8:11, 14, 17). The sermons of Deuteronomy call Israel to remember in every circumstance that dependence upon Yahweh is the source of her life. Hosea employs these characteristically Deuteronomic motifs: "Israel has forgotten his Maker" (8:14). The concept of "forget" is basic to the thought of covenant breaking in Hosea (see 4:6; 2:13; 13:6). It concerns a basic denial of what it means to be Israel.[22]

> Ephraim has said, "Ah, but I am rich,
>   I have gained wealth for myself" (12:8),

a phrase which closely follows Deuteronomy 8:17:

> ". . . Beware lest you say in your heart, 'My power and the might of my hand have gotten me this wealth.' You shall remember the LORD your God, for it is he who gives you power to get wealth; that he may confirm his covenant which he swore to your fathers, as at this day. And if you forget the LORD your God . . ."

This is echoed in Hosea 13:6:

> but when they had fed to the full,
>   they were filled, and their heart was lifted up;
>   therefore they forgot me.

For the parallel, see Deuteronomy 8:12-16:

> ". . . lest, when you have eaten and are full . . . then your heart
> be lifted up, and you forget the LORD your God, who brought you
> out of the land of Egypt, . . . who fed you in the wilderness with
> manna which your fathers did not know [cf. Hosea 13:5], that he
> might humble you and test you, to do you good in the end."

Hosea struggles with a people involved in a great cultural transition from a semi-nomadic to an agricultural life. Hosea summons Israel to face the crisis of the relevance of Yahweh for this culture. In this he reacts precisely as does Deuteronomy. Even in the new circumstance, Israel has no alternative but faith in Yahweh if she intends to be Israel.

A third recurring motif is the *attitude toward kingship*. Hosea, of all the prophets, gives attention to this problem, and Deuteronomy (17:14-20) alone of all the legal formulations considers this institution.[23] Thus a priori we expect affinities, and they are considerable. The law of Deuteronomy is concerned that the king be an Israelite who is steeped in the covenantal understanding of life and who subordinates his own interests to the covenant law. Hosea's persistent polemic against kingship is precisely in these terms:

> They made kings, but not through me.
>   They set up princes, but without my knowledge (8:4).

> Where now is your king, to save you;
>   where are all your princes, to defend you—
> those of whom you said,
>   "Give me a king and princes"?
> I have given you kings in my anger,
>   and I have taken them away in my wrath (13:10-11; cf. 5:10;
>   7:3, 7; 8:10b; 9:15; 10:3).

Hosea is not really interested in the institution of monarchy but in the covenantal foundations of the community, which can be understood only in terms of the older covenantal laws.[24] His point persistently is that in choosing kings and removing them, or having them removed, Israel has disregarded the real structure and authority of life, which is covenant under Yahweh. In yet another way, Israel has taken over non-Israelite practices.

Fourth among the general concerns of Hosea which reappear several times is the concern for *cultic legitimacy*. Israel is not to build shrines indiscriminately, nor to appropriate Canaanite sanctuaries together with their practices. Authorized shrines are those which are faithful to the covenant purposes of worship. Though the early provision (Exod. 20:24) had permitted numerous shrines, the legislation of Deuteronomy has severely limited this, not in the interest of a single shrine but in the interest of legitimate covenantal worship, free of pagan influences:

> "You shall surely destroy all the places where the nations whom you shall dispossess served their gods, upon the high mountains and upon the hills and under every green tree; you shall tear down their altars, and dash in pieces their pillars, and burn their Asherim with fire; you shall hew down the graven images of their gods, and destroy their name out of that place. You shall not do so to the LORD your God. But you shall seek the place which the LORD your God will choose . . ." (Deut. 12:2-5a; cf. Exod. 23:23-25).

Hosea indicts Israel because she has done just the opposite. She has not destroyed the Canaanite establishments and practices but has appropriated them. The whole establishment of shrines has not been for worship but for sin:

> They sacrifice on the tops of the mountains,
>   and make offerings upon the hills,
> under oak, poplar, and terebinth,
>   because their shade is good (4:13).

The passage continues with a discussion of cult prostitution.

> Because Ephraim has multiplied altars for sinning,
>   they have become to him altars for sinning (8:11).[25]

> The more his fruit increased
>   the more altars he built;
> as his country improved
>   he improved his pillars (10:1; cf. 4:19; 10:8).

The point of attack is not that there are too many shrines. The principle of exclusivism has been ignored. The old law has been violated and therefore covenant is broken.

(2) Specific Commandments Derived from Deuteronomy

In addition to the broad themes which show affinities between Hosea and Deuteronomy, specific parallels suggest close relationship between the ancient legal tradition and the prophecy of Hosea.

We may note first the relationships with the curse recital of Deuteronomy 27. In general these follow the pattern already noted with the decalogue. This includes the indictment concerning idols (Hosea 4:12, 17; 8:4; 11:2; 13:2) which is akin to Deuteronomy 27:15:

> "Cursed be the man who makes a graven or molten image, an abomination to the LORD, a thing made by the hands of a craftsman, and sets it up in secret."

A second curse is that of Deuteronomy 27:19:

> "Cursed be he who perverts the justice due to the sojourner, the fatherless, and the widow."

Though dependence is not demonstrable, the indictment of Hosea 10:13 should be noted:

> You have plowed iniquity,
>   you have reaped injustice,
>   you have eaten the fruit of lies.

The verbal relation is not precise, but the indictment of "iniquity" and "injustice" is a counterpart of "justice" in the curse pronouncement.

A third parallel is based on the curse of Deuteronomy 27:24, "Cursed be he who slays his neighbor in secret," and the indictment:

> As robbers lie in wait for a man,
>   so the priests are banded together;
> they murder on the way to Shechem,
>   yea, they commit villainy (Hosea 6:9).

In each case, the original curse formulation dealt with a very specific and concrete deed. Hosea deepens and extends them to become much more radical statements. Thus the warning about idols in Hosea becomes a judgment upon the character of all of life as it is linked to the notion of harlotry. The curse on perverting justice becomes a critique of political life. The warning on secret slaying becomes an attack upon cult which culminates in harlotry (6:10). Hosea uses these forms to make his primary point: Israel has violated covenant and so must bear the curse.

The exposition of this theme is carried further by his use of specific laws from Deuteronomy. The two motifs of sacred prostitution and ritual lament are employed to show how the worship of Israel has really become Canaanite. The old law on cultic prostitution asserts:

> "There shall be no cult prostitute of the daughters of Israel, neither shall there be a cult prostitute of the sons of Israel. You shall not bring the hire of a harlot, or the wages of a dog, into the house of the LORD your God in payment for any vow . . ." (Deut. 23:17-18).

These practices are an abomination to Yahweh, because they do not square with covenant faith. Hosea has the same motif.

> for the men themselves go aside with harlots,
> and sacrifice with cult prostitutes (4:14).

This particular link in Hosea 4 is one of many variations on the theme of harlotry and leads to one of his most devastating indictments. This is in keeping with the judgment of Deuteronomy 23:17-18, that it is an abomination to Yahweh.

General participation in Canaanite ritual practices is condemned in Deuteronomy 14:1-2:

> "You are the sons of the LORD your God; you shall not cut yourselves or make any baldness on your foreheads for the dead. For you are a people holy to the LORD your God . . ." (cf. Lev. 19:28).

To do this is a denial of the holiness of Israel and a forfeiture of a unique covenantal relationship. So also Hosea:

> They do not cry to me from the heart,
>   but they wail upon their beds;
> for grain and wine they gash themselves,
>   they rebel against me (7:14).

To participate in any such rite is to rebel against Yahweh, thereby denying covenant. It represents an attempt to control life and harness its powers for our own ends. Obviously, Yahweh will not countenance that.

From the laws which deal with commercial concerns, Hosea has derived two indictments:

> The princes of Judah have become
> like those who remove the landmark (5:10a).[26]

> A trader, in whose hands are false balances,
> he loves to oppress (12:7).

Deuteronomy offers good evidence for the legal basis of the indictment:

> ". . . you shall not remove your neighbor's landmark, which the men of old have set" (Deut. 19:14; cf. 27:17).

> "You shall not have in your bag two kinds of weights, a large and a small. You shall not have in your house two kinds of measures, a large and a small. A full and just weight you shall have, a full and just measure you shall have . . ." (Deut. 25:13-15).

The first of these is apodictic in formulation and the second concludes with a statement about abomination (Deut. 25:16). Both therefore make a very strong appeal. But Hosea extends them even farther. In the first of these (5:10) he takes a domestic law and uses it for a comment upon international politics. In the second (12:7) he transforms a prohibition maintaining honest commerce into an indictment upon the pride and self-sufficiency of Ephraim when she is intended to be dependent because of the Exodus event (12:9).

The profundity of Hosea's understanding of the sin of Israel and the breaking of covenant has a variety of sources. But it is clear from the evidence cited that he has fully entered into and has learned much from the tradition of Deuteronomy.

3. THE HARLOTRY MOTIF

Of all the figures which Hosea uses, it is clear that the image of the harlot is the most important. Here we wish only to show that this also is thoroughly grounded in the old legal tradition.[27] In the older traditions, it most often applies to specific violations of persons. By contrast in Hosea it has become a general figure for the whole covenant people. But this is the characteristic way in which Hosea handles the old traditions.

In the decalogue we have noted the term "adultery" which Hosea also used, but here our concern is with the term "harlotry." Perhaps the oldest of the legal formulations with this term, and certainly the fullest, is Exodus 34:14-16:

> ". . . (for you shall worship no other god, for the LORD, whose name is Jealous, is a jealous God), lest you make a covenant with the inhabitants of the land, and when they play the harlot after their gods and sacrifice to their gods and one invites you, you eat of his sacrifice, and you take of their daughters for your sons, and their daughters play the harlot after their gods and make your sons play the harlot after their gods."

This statement, in one of the oldest strata of the Pentateuch, is very similar to Deuteronomy 7 already cited. It does not refer to specific cases but to the covenant of people and God. The motif has as its counterpart the jealousy of Yahweh, which is central to Deuteronomy and less directly to the tradition of Hosea. It is the *exclusiveness* of Yahweh's covenant with Israel which has been violated. For this indictment the image of harlot is especially well-suited. In using the motif Hosea stands in the mainstream of covenant theology and can be appreciated only in this context.[28]

The other uses of the term in the legal materials include Leviticus 17:7; 20:5, 6; 21:7, 9, 14 from H and the clear statement of 19:29:

> "Do not profane your daughter by making her a harlot, lest the land fall into harlotry and the land become full of wickedness."

Here the law refers to a particular case but moves to make the more general covenantal statement. This unit ends with the supreme covenantal affirmation: "I am Yahweh." In Deuteronomy, strangely enough, the term occurs only in 22:21 and 23:18, but in both cases it is the identity, uniqueness, and purity of Israel which are at stake. Thus harlotry becomes for the various legal traditions a negative way of commenting upon the important question of covenant faithfulness.

The use of the term and the concept is, as is well known, pervasive in Hosea. (See 1:2; 2:4-5, 6, 7; 3:3; 4:10-18; 5:3-4; 6:10; 9:1.) It is the central thrust of the tradition of Hosea, as is evident in the hope passages which promise right relation and the end of harlotry:

> ". . . For I will remove the names of the Baals from her mouth, and they shall be mentioned by name no more. . . . And I will betroth you to me for ever; I will betroth you to me in righteousness and in justice, in steadfast love, and in mercy. I will betroth you to me in faithfulness; and you shall know the LORD" (2:17, 19-20).

The exclusive love relationship will be an end to all harlotry.

> O Ephraim, what have I to do with idols?
>   It is I who answer and look after you.
> I am like an evergreen cypress,
>   from me comes your fruit (14:8).

The use of fertility images indicates an awareness of the problem of harlotry. The prophet affirms that harlotry may now be eliminated because the supposed benefits of harlotry are now all available inside the relation of fidelity. The whole movement of broken covenant and restored covenant is set in the context of harlotry and jealousy, in which Hosea follows the older legal traditions.

Hosea understands more than the other eighth-century prophets the helplessness of Israel. (In the next century Jeremiah also had a profound grasp of the problem [13:23].) Hosea understood that even if Israel wanted to change and renew covenant, she was "caught" in a most desperate way. To speak of this trap, he uses the phrase "spirit of harlotry":

> For a spirit of harlotry has led them astray,
>   and they have left their God to play the harlot (4:12b; cf. 5:4b).

The plight of Israel is not due to isolated acts or deliberate covenant breaking. Something more than that has happened to Israel. There has been an urge which Israel has been unable to resist.[29] This drive toward unfaithfulness is the very antithesis of healthy covenant relation. Israel has fallen in love with another master and has forsaken Yahweh.

In 5:4b "spirit of harlotry" is set in opposition to "they know not Yahweh." The juxtaposition of the two phrases is a most insightful achievement. On the one hand, Israel is out of covenant with Yahweh. They do not acknowledge his lordship or his graciousness. On the other hand, Israel is beholden to another power, caught up in a way of life and an understanding of history which exclude Yahweh and all his claims. Israel always has the options of life and death (see Deut. 30:15-20). Here she has chosen death and there is no way back to life (see Isa. 28:15, 18).

Finally, the climactic phrase of 4:10 summarizes the image:

> Surely the LORD they have abandoned to heed harlotry.

The phrase is introduced by the powerful "surely," suggesting that this is the real point of the oracle. The line is chiastic, beginning with *Yahweh,* ending with *harlotry,* the two poles between which Israel always struggles. The center of the line involves two great verbs. To "abandon" is a covenant term widely used by Jeremiah. The counter term for "abandon" is "heed," one of the great words of Deuteronomy which implies the careful attention to all dimensions of covenant. Here the term is used ironically.

Israel has forsaken covenant. She has embraced nothingness. Israel has rejected life. She has chosen death. The response she was to make to Yahweh she now gives to "harlotry." The claims of the commandments are rejected in favor of another view of history. Instead of obedience, she has opted for self-indulgence and manipulation. It is as if to say, "They keep covenant with harlotry, they keep faith with faithlessness, they desert the real to woo the unreal."

The judgment is thoroughly grounded in the legal tradition. The crucial development in Hosea beyond the old traditions is that because of grace (11:8-9), the great indictment may be inverted:

Surely they abandon harlotry to heed Yahweh (cf. 14:1-8).

Hosea uses the old legal traditions to show the ground upon which Israel must live and the authority by which he speaks his word of indictment. Israel has not honored the covenant stipulations to which she pledged herself. In respect to both the historical and the legal traditions, it is clear that Hosea did not speak spontaneously what he chose. His total message is thoroughly grounded in the memories and conditions of the old covenant tradition. This vigorous and consistent use of the old traditions is the first link between the prophets and the community of faith in which they lived. It is the first line of evidence which summons us to a new understanding of the ministry of prophecy.

III.

The Prophets and the Covenant Forms

A second line of evidence argues for the close relationship between the prophets and the ancient covenant faith. The prophets have employed a variety of *forms* which necessarily assume the old traditions.[1] In the context of our modern romantic view of prophecy, in the Protestant churches we have generally assumed that the prophets were free spirits who spoke spontaneously, who gave structure and order to their oracles on the spur of the moment; i.e., everything they said was purely *ad hoc*. It is increasingly clear, however, that we are dealing not with emancipated men of the Renaissance, but with members of an ancient Oriental community who were largely dominated by the pressures, expectations, and practices of their community.

By our excessive concern for free form and unshackled expression of an uninhibited spirit, we have tended to ignore the rather fixed forms in which a speaker of the ancient Orient expressed himself. Characteristically he spoke in conventional forms, so that certain emotional nuances and tones of meaning were borne not only by certain words, but also by the arrangement of words and the employment of key words in recurring fashion. The prophet spoke this way not as an unhappy slave of a stereotype, but because this was the accepted mode of effective communication. For a society not yet perverted by extreme individualism, this was neither an unhappy nor an unimaginative way of speech. This is simply the way it was done, the way even the great masters of rhetoric spoke. To be sure, this did not exclude personal variations in speaking, nor reduce every prophet to the same mold. But it did set certain limits and boundaries to his work. By the recovery of these boundaries and patterns of speech we can discover a great deal about the intention of the speech as it is preserved, and about the way in which the prophets related to the old traditions.

In this chapter we will investigate the forms which are employed by Hosea. It seems clear that the prophet did indeed follow a fairly fixed pattern of speech. However, the form is less clear in Hosea than in almost any other prophet.[2] This means that we will most often find only fragments of form. But where the fragments occur, it is essential to envision the entire form so that the fragment may be understood according to its original intention. In studying these forms we will want to pay particular attention to connections with the old covenant traditions and the legal commitments of covenant which they assume.

The Forms of Prophetic Speech

There are many diverse forms in prophetic oracles.[3] It is not our purpose to explore all of these but only to indicate the ways in which discernment of form is an indispensable tool for interpretation. We will limit our discussion to the four elements which are most often regarded as basic to prophetic proclamation.

1. THE SPEECH OF JUDGMENT

The most characteristic form in the pre-exilic prophets serves to *indict* Israel for her violation of covenant commitments and pronounce *sentence* because of her infidelity. It is on the basis of the indictment that the sentence is announced. The two elements bear something like a cause and effect relationship. The two motifs may be distinguished for purposes of analysis. They may at times stand independent of each other because of the fragmentation of form. However, the forms belong together in their logical construction and cannot be properly understood apart from each other. The two together, indictment and sentence, form the "speech of judgment."

(1) The Indictment

The first form which concerns us is the indictment. With this form the prophet declares to Israel that she has sinned and has violated the covenant. Because he intends to establish the guilt of the covenant people, he offers a bill of particulars showing precisely and in what ways Israel has sinned and broken covenant. Thus the indictment speech is often directly related to a law of the ancient covenantal legal tradition. The indictment makes no sense at all without some prior legal precedents. In Israel these are most plausibly to be located in the stipulations of the covenant. Such reference to the old tradition means that the prophet does not freely and capriciously make wild accusations against Israel. Rather the indictments are carefully prepared charges grounded in legal requirements to which Israel has given formal assent. Though the indictments have general implications, the accusation itself is characteristically specific and well defined. The relation of the form to the old tradition can be formulated in this way:

(a) The old covenant law defined requirements about what must be done and what may not be done.

(b) The indictment form asserts the guilt of Israel and appeals to the precedents of the old tradition.

Unfortunately the form in Hosea is not as clear as we might wish.[4] However, there are enough clues to provide a basis for seeking to reconstruct the full form. It apparently would contain the following elements:

A summons to hear, an imperative.
The naming of the accused.
The naming of the accuser.
Announcement of trial.
A general accusation.
A more specific listing.

The only clear and fairly complete example of the indictment in Hosea is in 4:1-2:

Summons to hear:	Hear the word of the LORD,
Name of accused:	O people of Israel . . .
	inhabitants of the land.
Name of accuser:	For the LORD
Announcement of trial:	has a controversy . . .
General accusation:	There is no faithfulness or kindness, and no knowledge of God in the land;

More specific listing: there is swearing, lying, killing,
                          stealing, and committing adultery;
                          they break all bounds and murder
                          follows murder.

When the form has been delineated, we may ask more precisely
about the relation to the old tradition. There can be no doubt that
the specific list of charges alludes to the decalogue (Exod. 20:2-17;
Deut. 5:6-21). Because of the specific charges rooted in the tradition to which Israel has given assent, the more general indictment
of 1b is cogent.[5]

A second good example of the form occurs in 6:7-10, though
already some elements are lacking. Instead of proper names, now
pronouns for the two parties are employed:

Name of accused: they transgressed . . .
Name of accuser: me.
Announcement of trial: they transgressed the covenant.
General accusation: they dealt faithlessly with me.
More specific listing: Gilead is a city of evildoers,
                        tracked with blood.
                        As robbers lie in wait for a man,
                        so the priests are banded together;
                        they murder on the way to She-
                        chem,
                        yea, they commit villainy.[6]

Verse 10 functions as a kind of reprise, for it reasserts the reference
to the accused and the accuser and again makes a general statement of guilt. A study of the specific indictments indicates that we
have a charge carefully formulated in light of the laws and moving
toward a clear statement of guilt.

A third example of the indictment which builds upon legal
precedent is in 8:4:

Name of accused: They . . .
Name of accuser: me.
General accusation: They made kings . . .
                       They set up princes . . .
Specific listing: With their silver and gold they made
                           idols
                       for their own destruction.

Perhaps the specific listing is not an accurate development of the general statement, but it is not to be regarded as a careless departure from form. It rather indicates the way an indictment builds so that the general statement can move in several directions. The legal precedent behind this indictment is most likely in Deuteronomy 17:14-17, but it also plays upon the frequent prohibitions on images and idols. The linking of the two makes a more telling attack on the political disorder and irresponsibility of the time.

In 9:1 we again meet with a summons to hear, though stated in a slightly different way:

Summons to hear:	Rejoice not . . .
	Exult not like the peoples . . .
Name of the accused:	O Israel!
Name of accuser:	your God
General accusation:	you have played the harlot . . .
Specific listing:	You have loved a harlot's hire
	upon all threshing floors.

Two specific references to the old tradition may be found here: one is the harlotry of syncretism (Exod. 34:11-16; Deut. 7:1-5). The second, which is more specific, is the practice of cult prostitution (Deut. 23:17-18).

A slightly different use of the form is apparent in 11:12—12:2.

Name of accused:	Ephraim . . . Israel
Name of accuser:	me
General accusation:	encompassed . . . with lies,
	. . . with deceit;[7]
Specific listing:	Ephraim herds the wind,
	and pursues the east wind all day long;
	they multiply falsehood and violence;
	they make a bargain with Assyria,
	and oil is carried to Egypt.
Announcement of trial:	The LORD has an indictment against Judah,[8] and will punish Jacob according to his ways.

The form is broken in Hosea to an exceptional extent. This means that often we do not find the consistent form but only clues

to it. Where the clues are evident, proper interpretation requires
that we "hear" the entire form. Thus the summons to court expressed in the imperative "Hear" (cf. 4:1 and less directly 9:1) is
used in 5:1 with the naming of the accused and the announcement
of the trial (cf. Amos 3:1, 13; 4:1; Micah 1:2; 3:1, 9). Frequently the actual statement of accusation is introduced by the
strong particle "for" ("surely"), which is an assertion of vigor
and certainty, an oath-like expression that the accusation is true.[9]
We have seen this in 4:1 and 9:1. Often the indictment with this
form of introduction and identification follows the sentence and so
serves as a basis for the sentence which has already been given:[10]

> Surely you have rejected knowledge . . .
> and . . . you have forgotten the law [Torah] of your God (4:6).

> Surely they have forsaken the LORD to cherish harlotry (4:10).

Though brief, this unit names the accused and accuser, gives a
general accusation, and prepares for the specifics in verses 11-13.
Notice in each of these the naming of the accuser. The accused is
at times referred to in the second person and sometimes in the
third, but this has no particular significance.

Other examples of the indictment introduced with this decisive
particle include:

> Surely the men themselves go aside with harlots,
>   and sacrifice with cult prostitutes (4:14).

> Surely like a stubborn heifer,
>   Israel is stubborn (4:16).

> Surely they have borne alien children (5:7b; cf. 9:1; 10:13).

In addition to the particle, these fragments only name the accused
and give the general accusation.

On some occasions the indictment is recognized primarily because the accused is named. See 4:12 (my people); 7:8, 11, and
12:8 (Ephraim); Deuteronomy 32:15 (Jeshurun). Sometimes
even the name is absent. When this happens it indicates a very
deliberate use of the form, for the indictment is hardened by the
cold, impersonal use of "they" (6:7; 7:14; 8:4, 7) which suggests

the deep brokenness of the covenant relationship. The form is no less clear, but the prophet introduces a clear emotive flavor by refusing the formal legal pattern of naming the defendant. The indictment stated in such a way expresses Yahweh's detachment from his unfaithful people.

With the form thus clearly established in Hosea, we may note other rather abrupt and fragmented examples:

> They turn to Baal (7:16).[12]

This indictment is followed by a specific which refers to "insolence of their tongue."

> Israel has spurned the good (8:3).[13]
> Israel has forgotten his Maker (8:14).

This is followed by specifics which refer to building palaces and fortifying cities.

> They utter mere words (10:4; cf. Deut. 32:15).

This very abrupt quality which retains only a fragment of the original form is strengthened and made more urgent by the addition of the particle "now."[14]

> Surely now, O Ephraim, you have played the harlot (5:3).
> And now they sin more and more . . . (13:2).

This general accusation in 13:2 is well filled out with specific listing:

> . . . and make for themselves molten images,
> idols skilfully made of their silver,
>   all of them the work of craftsmen.
> Sacrifice to these, they say.
>   Men kiss calves!

Here the specifics function very effectively to define the general accusation, of which the meaning is not clear. This is precisely what is needed in a legal context where indictments cannot be sustained on vague and ill-defined grounds.

The message of each of the indictments is that Israel is guilty of having broken covenant. The link to the old covenant tradition is clear. Unless there is a legal tradition to which the prophet can make appeal, the accusations are nonsense. The form as such requires the assumption of appeal to some such tradition.

(2) The Sentence

When the accused has been indicted the next step in the procedure is to pronounce the sentence. Scholarship has moved away from the term "threat" because that word suggests anger or vengeance. When the prophetic form is understood not to be an emotional attack upon the guilty party, then the term "threat" becomes inappropriate.[15] Punishment must come to Israel because she has been unfaithful to the covenant. The sentence is the way in which the prophets announce God's verdict upon the covenant violator.

As in the case of the indictments, so also in the sentences, the prophetic form appeals to the traditional covenant forms. We have shown in chapter one that the recital of blessings and curses is an integral part of the initial covenant ceremony. The curses are guaranteed to fall upon all who betray covenant by violating its conditions. The sentence which the prophet announces upon the heels of the indictment is in fact the execution of the covenant curses known from the beginning of the covenant relation.[16] The relationship of curse and sentence may be stated in this way:

     (a) The covenant curse announced what would happen to offenders of covenant.

     (b) The prophets, having determined the guilt of Israel, announce again the curses which must now come upon the party found guilty.[17]

Of the various curses in the Old Testament, the two great recitals are in Leviticus 26 and Deuteronomy 28.[18] Though the finished form of these chapters may be later, both in structure and in substance they belong to the earliest expression of Israel's covenant liturgy. They are clearly assumed by the prophets. The prophetic sentences make better sense with these in mind. Without this kind of curse tradition which has previously been sanctioned in Israel, the prophetic sentences are difficult to understand and impossible to accept.

The form of the sentence is noticeably barren in Hosea. There are no "announcement formulae" as in the other prophets. There is only the statement of the punishment to come and occasionally a statement of the agent by which the punishment will come. Sometimes there is also a description of the people after the sentence has been executed.

Westermann[19] draws the conclusion that the pure form of sentence is the statement about punishment. There are ample examples of that in Hosea. However, there are also numerous examples of sentences in which the intervention of God is taken as a part of the sentence with the first person pronoun. Yet a third variety appears when an agent is named who will bring the punishment. In 10:10 all three come together:

divine intervention:	I will come against the wayward people to chastise them;
agent:	and nations shall be gathered against them
simple description:	when they are chastised for their double iniquity.

While a distinction can be made in the three ways of speaking and sentence *qua* sentence requires only the third element, I find no evidence which makes one secondary or additional. These appear to be three equally valid ways of introducing the sentence to the accused. Moreover the appeal to the old curses of Leviticus 26 and Deuteronomy 28 sustains the judgment that divine intervention is an integral part of the form, for that already appears in the curse recital.[20] It is risky to give priority to one way of speaking about the threat because they all bear for Israel a similar message and this message can scarcely be understood apart from the activity of the covenant Lord. A fourth element in the form which appears in Hosea with some regularity is the allusion to the indictment which is not a separate form but an element in this form (see 4:9; 7:12; 10:15). Thus in 10:10 just cited, it concludes with a reference to "their double iniquity." Such a device helps tie the sentence closely to the indictment.

The sentences which follow Westermann's purest form include the following:

> You shall stumble by day,
>> the prophet also shall stumble with you by night (4:5);

but it is followed immediately with an "I-speech":

> and I will destroy your mother (4:5).

Another example shows a combination:

> Ephraim shall stumble in his guilt;
> Judah also shall stumble with them,

but this form includes a reference to Yahweh:

> he has withdrawn from them,

and mention of an agent:

> Now the new moon shall devour them with their fields (5:5b-7).

A pure example is found in 14:1:

> . . . surely you have stumbled.

This is followed by an allusion to the indictment:

> . . . because of your iniquity.

A simple form is also apparent in 8:6:

> The calf of Samaria
>> shall be broken to pieces.

We encounter a characteristic element in 13:3, again with Westermann's simple form:

> Therefore they shall be like the morning mist
>> or like the dew that goes early away,
> like the chaff that swirls from the threshing floor
>> or like smoke from a window.

The initial word, "therefore," is common in the form and serves to link the sentence to the indictment.[21]

A variation in the form, though not an expansion, is the sentence announced in terms of divine intervention. We have already mentioned the uses of 4:5 and 10:10. Others are the following:

> Surely I will be like a lion to Ephraim . . .
> I, even I, will rend and go away,
>> I will carry off, and none shall rescue (5:14).

> ... but I will send a fire upon his cities,
> and it shall devour his strongholds (8: 14).

In this passage another agent is given in the final lines of the unit.

> Therefore I will hedge up her way with thorns;
> and I will build a wall against her (2:6).

> Therefore I will take back
> my grain in its time,
> and my wine in its season;
> and I will take away my wool and my flax ...
> Now I will uncover her lewdness
> in the sight of her lovers ...
> And I will put an end to all her mirth ...
> And I will lay waste her vines and her fig trees ...
> I will make them a forest ...
> And I will punish her for the feast days of the Baals ... (2:9-13).

> So I will be to them like a lion,
> like a leopard I will lurk beside the way.
> I will fall upon them like a bear robbed of her cubs,
> I will tear open their breast,
> and there I will devour them like a lion,
> as a wild beast would rend them (13:7-8).

Yet a third way of putting the sentence is to allude to an agent who will bring the punishment. We have mentioned those in 8:14 and 10:10. Others include:

> Aliens devour his strength ... (7:9).
> their princes shall fall by the sword (7:16).
> therefore the tumult of war shall arise among your people ...
> (10:14).

> The sword shall rage against their cities,
> consume the bars of their gates,
> and devour them in their fortresses (11:6).

> they shall fall by the sword ... (13:16).

The form has a great deal of freedom. While the simple announcement is one way of putting the sentence, it is not the only or the preferred way of putting it. To claim that is to cut it off from the curse tradition to which it is securely attached, as Westermann himself admits.

The evidence for connections with the curse tradition is abundant.

(1) The notion that God will chastise the guilty (Hosea 5:2b; 10:10) is linked to the curse of Leviticus 26:18, 28:

> ". . . then I will chastise you again sevenfold for your sins . . ."

(2) The idea that the unfaithful will stumble (4:5; 5:5b) is an echo of the curse of Leviticus 26:37:

> "They shall stumble over one another, as if to escape a sword, though none pursues . . ."

(3) More specifically, one way of executing the sentence is the sword, i.e., military invasion (7:16; 11:6; 13:16). The sword is mentioned in an "I-speech" in Leviticus 26:25:

> "And I will bring a sword upon you, that shall execute vengeance for the covenant."

(4) Another agent of the sentence is the lion (5:14; 13:7-8), as a simile which is perhaps related to the curse of wild animals:[22]

> "And I will let loose the wild beasts among you, which shall rob you of your children, and destroy your cattle, and make you few in number, so that your ways shall become desolate" (Lev. 26:22).

(5) Allusions to food and eating (4:10) have close parallel to the curse of Leviticus 26:26:

> ". . . and you shall eat, and not be satisfied."

Loss of food to enemies (7:9; 8:7) also has a parallel in the curse recital:

> "And you shall sow your seed in vain, for your enemies shall eat it" (Lev. 26:16; cf. Deut. 28:33).

(6) Destruction is a common motif in the sentence form in Hosea (8:6, 14; 10:14; 11:6). While the parallel is not so precise, it may not be unrelated:

> "And I will destroy your high places, and cut down your incense altars, and cast your dead bodies upon the dead bodies of your idols; and my soul will abhor you. And I will lay your cities waste,

and will make your sanctuaries desolate, and I will not smell your pleasing odors" (Lev. 26:30-31).

This last curse implies a rejection of perverted cult; see also Hosea 4:19; 8:13; 10:2, 8.

(7) There are allusions to exile (4:19; 8:10; 9:3, 15, 17; 10:6), which have a counterpart in Deuteronomy 28:64:

"And the LORD will scatter you among all peoples, from one end of the earth to the other . . ." (cf. Lev. 26:33).[23]

(8) Pursuit by the enemy is threatened in Hosea 8:3 in a way which recalls Deuteronomy 28:25:

". . . you shall go out one way against them, and flee seven ways before them . . ."

(9) The cursed, sentenced people will become a derision to their neighbors (7:16). This is very similar to the curse of Deuteronomy 28:37:

"And you shall become a horror, a proverb, and a byword, among all the peoples where the LORD will lead you away."

There are, of course, other sentences in Hosea which have no apparent relation to either of the great curse collections. These include dry rot and moth (5:12), fire (8:14), miscarriage and dry breasts (9:14), eating unclean food (9:3), being caught in a net (7:12), and thistles and thorns (10:8).

The sentence form may appear in several ways, but each time it serves to announce the penalty upon the guilty party. The way in which the sentence is announced varies in its form, but the variants share the assumption that violation of covenant brings such penalties. The parallels with the old curses which we have cited do not illuminate the form as such. But they do suggest the background to which the sentences appeal.[24] We have seen that the indictment is not capricious or *ad hoc* but by definition makes appeal to a legal tradition. In a similar way the sentences are not off-the-cuff threats but make appeal to a clearly defined legal tradition. Once it is clear that we are dealing with legal forms, it follows that we must posit a tradition behind the form. Although not necessarily the case, it is most plausible that in both indictments and sentences the prophet appeals to the covenant tradition.

In Hosea the full introduction of the announcement does not appear. We have suggested that the "therefore" may function in a similar way in Hosea. However, even this indication is not always used. The poetry of Hosea is saturated with the form, but often the standard clues are missing. A proper reading of the prophet requires that the form be recognized where its set pattern cannot be discerned. Sometimes formal elements can help us to locate them. The variation in Hosea is endless, but among the more noteworthy ways of beginning the pronouncement of a sentence are these:

(a) With a verb, which makes it abrupt:

A wind has *wrapped* them in its wings,
    and they shall be ashamed because of their altars (4:19).

their princes shall *fall* by the sword (7:16; cf. 8:8; 9:16; 10:7; 11:6).

(b) With a noun, which also is rather abrupt:

The enemy shall pursue him (8:3).
Threshing floor and winevat shall not feed them . . . (9:2).

(c) Occasionally the sentence begins by naming the party to be punished:

Ephraim shall become a desolation
    in the day of punishment (5:9; cf. 9:11).

(d) A variety of particles may also be employed. Among the most used is "surely," closely related to "therefore":

Surely I will be like a lion to Ephraim,
    and like a young lion to the house of Judah (5:14).

Surely the calf of Samaria
    shall be broken to pieces (8:6b).

Surely if they bring up children,
    I will bereave them till none is left (9:12; cf. 8:7).

This form may be strengthened even more by the combination "for behold":

For behold, they are going to Assyria (9:6).

(e) A like usage is with "now," which stresses the immediance of the sentence:

Now the new moon shall devour them with their fields (5:7).

Now I will gather them up.
And they shall cease for a little while
from anointing king and princes (8:10).

Now they must bear their guilt (10:2; cf. 8:13).

(f) In a weaker form, the sentence may be introduced with a simple conjunction which in this context may best be translated "therefore," again in keeping with the above usage of "therefore":

Therefore I am like a moth to Ephraim,
and like dry rot to the house of Judah (5:12).

Therefore I will send a fire upon his cities,
and it shall devour his strongholds (8:14b; cf. 10:14; 12:14).

(g) A more certain marking is the occurrence of "woe" at the beginning, which certainly culminates in a threat:

Woe to them . . .
Destruction to them . . . (7:13; cf. 9:12).[25]

The sentence-form serves to determine the destiny of Israel in her times of harlotry. It may be expressed in many ways. But the form is characteristically a response to the indictment. Guilt must be punished. The form makes this announcement specific.

The prophet and his people assumed that keeping or violating covenant determined whether the community would receive the blessings or curses of covenant. These blessings and curses were not "spiritual" or "religious," but were concerned with the socio-economic, political, and material welfare of the community. For that reason they are taken with great seriousness. The prophetic sentences are the implementation of the curses upon Israel in her moments of disobedience. The sentences then are concerned with the misery and suffering and perhaps annihilation of Israel which were the sure result of covenant violation.

In the church today, there is great uncertainty about the propriety of pronouncing doom upon the community of faith when it is remiss in the demands of covenant. The analysis of prophetic speech does not resolve that difficult question. But it does suggest that "prophetic preaching" is not to be confused with anger and undisciplined denunciation. Rather, prophetic preaching is disciplined and precise in its appeal to traditions known by both preacher and listeners. Without this disciplined appeal to tradition, prophetic denunciation may have more to do with personal angers and frustrations than with the history of God's people.

(3) The Completed Speech of Judgment

For the purposes of analysis we have isolated the indictment and sentence as possessing their own properties, serving separate functions, each being rooted in the covenant tradition. Now we may note the way in which they belong together. We do not have two separate forms but a single form with two distinct parts. The completed form, composed of the indictment and sentence, is the most characteristic speech of the pre-exilic prophets. It declares to Israel that the covenant has been broken by an unresponsive people and that the brokenness of covenant must be punished by the God who offered and guaranteed the covenant. The two parts belong together like cause and effect, or conduct and consequence.[26] They have relationship precisely like the relation of law and curse in the liturgy:

A. The liturgy of covenant:
   1. These stipulations you shall obey . . . (e.g., Exod. 21:1—23:19; Lev. 26:1-2).
   2. Those who do not honor these laws will receive these punishments . . . (e.g., Exod. 23:20-21; Lev. 26:14-39).

B. The speech of judgment in the prophets:
   1. Surely you have not obeyed these stipulations . . .
   2. Therefore these judgments will come upon you . . .

The forms of indictment and sentence surely do emerge from a judicial context, as Westermann has argued. But as they stand in the prophets they have reference to the covenant commitments and curses which we now have in the old traditions. Thus the form functions to relate the present circumstance to that old tradition.

The judgment speech of 4:1-3 functions as the best example of this connection in Hosea:

Summons to hear:	Hear the word of the LORD,
Name of accused:	O people of Israel . . . inhabitants of the land.
Name of accuser:	Surely the LORD
Announcement of trial:	has a controversy . . .
General accusation:	There is no faithfulness or kindness, and no knowledge of God in the land;
Specific listing:	there is swearing, lying, killing, stealing, and committing adultery;
	they break all bounds and murder follows murder.
Formula of announcement:	Therefore . . .
Declaration of penalty:	the land mourns . . . and also the beasts of the field, and the birds of the air; and even the fish of the sea are taken away.

The summons to hear sets the oracle in the Lord-people context of covenant. The indictment recalls the old covenant stipulations known in the Torah. The sentence announces the penalty of the old curses upon those who are unfaithful to covenant. The forms in their present function make sense only as they refer back to the tradition of Moses.

2. ORACLE OF PROMISE: SALVATION ORACLE

The prophets are not only prosecuting attorneys for Yahweh against his wayward people; they are also spokesmen for the covenant, and as such they speak about every dimension of the covenant relation. They speak not only about broken covenant as in the case of the judgment speech, but also about the restored covenant. The covenant can be restored in one of two ways. (a) Israel can leave off her infidelity and return to Yahweh. (b) Yahweh in his graciousness can announce a fresh relationship in spite

of Israel's infidelity. Each of these possible ways of restoring covenant is expressed in a suitable form. The action whereby Yahweh
announces a fresh relationship in spite of Israel's infidelity is embodied in the oracle of promise or salvation oracle. This form
occurs only rarely in the eighth-century prophets and when it does
it causes great problems for analysis, for the form hardly seems
appropriate to the general tone of these traditions. Moreover, the
connection with the old covenant tradition is not so clear. Nevertheless we will examine the data contained in the Hosea tradition
which bear upon a possible relation.

This form has been most clearly outlined by Westermann, and
we will use the terminology he has introduced.[27] From his analysis
it is clear here as elsewhere that the prophet does not speak *ad hoc,*
but his assertions about restored covenant are disciplined by the
conventional expressions. The clearest expression of the form is
in 14:4-7:

announcement:[28]   I will heal their faithlessness;
                        I will love them freely . . .
                        I will be as the dew to Israel;
portrayal:[29]   He shall blossom as the lily,
                        he shall strike root as the poplar;
                        his shoots shall spread out;
                        his beauty shall be like the olive,
                        and his fragrance like Lebanon.
                        They shall return and dwell beneath
                            my shadow,
                        they shall flourish as a garden;
                        they shall blossom as the vine,
                        their fragrance shall be like the wine
                            of Lebanon.

The movement from the one way of speaking to the other is natural
and scarcely needs comment. Both announcement and portrayal
introduce us to a new situation where the covenant relation is completely restored.

The same inversion of situation is apparent in the magnificent
oracle of 2:14 ff.:

    Therefore, behold,[30]

assurance:[31]	I will allure her, I will bring her to the wilderness, I will speak tenderly to her. I will give her her vineyards from there, and make the Valley of Achor a door of hope.
portrayal:	And there she shall answer as in the days of her youth, as at the time when she came out of the land of Egypt.
portrayal:	*And in that day*, says the LORD, you will call me, "My husband," and no longer will you call me, "My Baal."
assurance:	I will remove the names of the Baals from her mouth, and they shall be mentioned by name no more. I will make for you a covenant on that day with the beasts of the field, the birds of the air, and the creeping things of the ground; I will abolish the bow, the sword, and war from the land; I will make you lie down in safety. I will betroth you to me for ever; I will betroth you to me in righteousness and in justice, in steadfast love, and in mercy. I will betroth you to me in faithfulness;
covenant formula:[32]	you shall know the LORD.
announcement:	*In that day*, says the LORD, I will answer the heavens
portrayal:	and they shall answer the earth; and the earth shall answer the grain, the wine, and the oil, and they shall answer Jezreel;

assurance: I will sow him for myself in the
                        land.
                        I will have pity on Not pitied,
                        I will say to Not my people, "You
                        are my people";
covenant formula: and he shall say, "Thou art my
                        God."

This unit, which is crucial to Hosea, is a good example of his
use of form. He relies here much less on the portrayal which we
saw in 14:5-7, and the announcement occurs almost incidentally.
In what is almost a chiastic structure he relies at beginning and
end on the assurance form. This is heightened even more by the
"covenant formula" at two crucial points in the total unit. As we
will see in our later discussion of the passage, this structure set
against 2:2-13 makes the theme of reversal decisive and unmis-
takable.

In 1:7 there is a promise-speech which is commonly regarded
as an intrusion in the text. It includes two imperfect verbs and
one in the perfect. Following Westermann's terminology it may
be analyzed in the following elements:

announcement: But I will have pity on the house of Judah . . .
assurance: I will deliver them by the LORD their God;
announcement: I will not deliver them by bow, nor by sword,
                nor by war, nor by horses, nor by horse-
                men.

In a moment we will consider the appeal to tradition made in this
unit. The progression of verbs from an imperfect to converted
perfect to imperfect suggests the movement and stress of the unit.
The entire statement stands at a curious place in the Hosea materials, but its affirmation is quite in keeping with the tradition
which stands behind Hosea. Perhaps the form offers a clue to the
setting for salvation-speeches throughout Hosea.

Another interesting structure occurs in the promise-oracle of
11:10-11:

portrayal: They shall go after the LORD,
             he will roar like a lion;
             yea, he will roar,

> and his sons shall come trembling from the west;
> they shall come trembling like birds from Egypt,
> and like doves from the land of Assyria;

assurance: and I will return them to their homes, says the
              LORD.

The construction shows again that the stress falls upon the assurance. This is indicated by the placement of the line as well as the concluding formula, "says the LORD." This does not mean that the preceding portrayal is unimportant but that the prophet reserves the assurance for his decisive declarations.

Finally the promise speech of 3:5 shows breakdown in the form:

> *Afterward*[33]

portrayal: the children of Israel shall return
              they shall seek the LORD their God, and David
                  their king;
              they shall come in fear to the LORD and to his
                  goodness

in the latter days.

It is clear that this describes a new situation of restored covenant. This is guaranteed by the use of "good," which refers to all the benefits and blessings of right covenant relation. But this unit moves considerably away from salvation speech, even though that influence is still strong, and moves toward a call to repentance. The classic words "seek" and "turn" from that form are present here, so that this is a mixture of forms. Perhaps this unit can be viewed as a remarkable synthesis in which Yahweh's announcement of a new relation and Israel's turning back to Yahweh are here combined with good effect. If so, this is an example of a message which requires ingenious handling of the conventional forms.

The use of the form needs little comment. The portrayal-speech, as Westermann indicates, employs the language of creation. This is remarkable in Hosea because it leads him into the very language of fertility religion which he means to attack. Thus the use of this form is an act of boldness on his part. No significant distinction can be made between the announcement and assurance, except to note that in the places which call for the strongest and climactic affirmations he has used the assurance form. These together with the "covenant formula" show that the prophet wishes not only to announce a new beginning to come but also to bring it into sharp and clear contrast with the old order of brokenness and infidelity.

Numerous motifs in these promise-speeches recall elements of the old blessing formulae:

(1) In 14:4-7 the general theme of wholeness is apparent.

(a) In verse 4, the prophetic promise is for healing and love.[34] In the blessing recital this is akin to Leviticus 26:11-12:

> "And I will make my abode among you, and my soul shall not abhor you. And I will walk among you, and will be your God, and you shall be my people" (cf. Deut. 28:9).

Thus the speech in Hosea 14 is a comment on covenant renewal.

(b) The language of fertility pervades these oracles, e.g., 14:5-7. This is reminiscent of Leviticus 26:4-5:

> ". . . then I will give you your rains in their season, and the land shall yield its increase, and the trees of the field shall yield their fruit. And your threshing shall last to the time of vintage, and the vintage shall last to the time for sowing; and you shall eat your bread to the full, and dwell in your land securely" (cf. Deut. 28:4-5, 8).

(c) A third idea in 14:4-7 is that of protection through God's presence. This same motif is found in Leviticus 26:5 just quoted and in verses 11-12 above and in verse 6:

> "And I will give peace in the land, and you shall lie down, and none shall make you afraid" (cf. Deut. 28:7).

(2) The promise-speech of 2:14-20 contains similar links to the tradition.

(a) Verses 14-15 are concerned with renewal of covenant and quickly move to the question of fertility. This sounds strikingly like the blessing formulae of Leviticus 26:4-12:

> "And I will have regard for you and make you fruitful and multiply you, and will confirm my covenant with you" (26:9).

(b) This oracle is concerned with the exclusiveness of Yahweh and the rejection of any attention for Baal (2:16-17). In a similar way the old tradition insisted on the exclusive claim of Yahweh (Lev. 26:12; Deut. 28:9-10).

(c) 2:18 refers to positive relations with other elements of creation. This promise is an approximate inversion of the covenant curses of Hosea 4:3. Perhaps this same concern is behind the promise of Leviticus 26:6 that evil beasts will be removed from the land.

(d) The promise of peace in verse 18 clearly has covenantal roots:

> "And I will give peace in the land, and you shall lie down, and none shall make you afraid . . . and the sword shall not go through your land" (Lev. 26:6).

There is in Hosea 2:18-20 a progression of (a) *harmony* in "nature" to (b) *peace* among peoples and finally (c) *wholesome covenant* relation with Yahweh. This sequence of concerns is probably derived from the old covenant tradition. The prophet, as the old tradition, skillfully draws together the motifs of covenant and fertility which answered a major temptation of the time and situation.

(3) The brief assertion of 1:7 is concerned with national security and success. This could quite easily be related to Leviticus 26:6-8, which also speaks of the defeat of the enemy. The relation between the covenant liturgy and the institution of Holy War is a very difficult question. There is, however, no question that they are in some way related. Thus it is quite possible that the blessing recital of Leviticus 26 has behind it, among other things, a Holy War tradition which is echoed in Hosea.[35]

(4) The inclusive promise of 11:10-11 suggests Yahweh's ability to control all of history and confound other nations for the sake of his covenant people. The old tradition includes a similar anticipation:

> "And all the peoples of the earth shall see that you are called by the name of the LORD; and they shall be afraid of you" (Deut. 28:10).

Similarly Leviticus 26:5 guarantees a secure land. Both Deuteronomy 28:10 and Leviticus 26:5 have a concern common to our passage. It may be that our passage is a late intrusion in the tradition, but even so, it indicates the remarkable fluidity with which the old tradition could be handled.

As we have seen with the other forms in Hosea, there are not many formal elements which help to identify the forms. In addition to the first person pronoun, there is the phrase "in that day" which occurs several times (2:16, 18, 21). This formula helps to draw the contrast between old brokenness and new restoration.

Thus far we have examined the form and have in general followed Westermann's categories. We have discovered in several places an additional element which stresses the covenant context. We have also found remarkable parallels with the old tradition of blessing recital. Though it cannot be proven beyond doubt, it seems likely that we can draw an additional conclusion from these forms and parallels in motif. It is most plausible that the prophet in using set forms is not supplying original content. Most likely he is appealing to a blessing tradition. If that is true, then it follows most naturally that the tradition to which he appeals is the covenant recital preserved in the places we have cited. In addition to the parallel in content, the parallel in form points toward this conclusion. There also the blessings belong to the covenant context and there also they are expressed in "I-speeches." The "I-speech" is of great importance because it serves to protest against the syncretistic notion that blessings come automatically or through the manipulation of gods and natural forces. Blessings come because Yahweh gives them.

Though Hosea uses the form, it is handled in a remarkable way. In the old recitals of Leviticus 26 and Deuteronomy 28, the blessings are promised in connection with obedience to covenant. Thus covenant theology as expressed in the recitals is a retribution theology. Only by faithfulness can Israel receive blessings. But in Hosea there is an important discontinuity between Israel's actions and the reception of blessing. The second does not follow from the first. Hosea has gone to great lengths to establish the infidelity of the covenant people. So the prophet appeals to a remarkable *non sequitur* in his use of this standard form. He preserves the form but makes it a vehicle for a quite different theological affirmation. Blessings do come to the disobedient.

Covenant promises are fulfilled for covenant violators. The promises of Hosea 2 and 14 come not as a result of obedience but in spite of disobedience. In Hosea, then, promises are grounded not in Israel's response but in Yahweh's initiating action, which is grace. The gracious gifts assured by the prophet derive not from what Israel does but from who Yahweh is.

The grounding of the promise in grace rather than in obedience is not a complete departure from the old covenant liturgy, but it does represent a new emphasis. It is evident in each of these units. In 2:14-20 only once (vs. 15) is there a suggestion of obedience as a condition, when it is said, "she shall answer as in the days of her youth." Yahweh's graciousness is fully expressed in the many uses of the verb in the first person with Yahweh as subject. "*I* will remove the names of the Baals." "*I* will make for you a covenant." "*I* will abolish the bow." "*I* will betroth you." Yahweh's relation to Israel is grounded in his promise. Though covenant-obedience is called for, it is not the basis of the relationship. Thus failure to obey does not void the relation. It is sustained by Yahweh's powerful graciousness even when Israel fails to respond.[36]

In 14:4, this note is sounded more briefly: "I will love them freely"; i.e., not according to a previous vow, not because he is compelled by any obligation, but spontaneously, out of his own passion for Israel. The promise motif, which is derived from the blessing of the covenant liturgy, here goes beyond the conventional relation of oath and blessing to give a quite different character to the relation. This receives its most complete affirmation in 11:9:

> I will not execute my fierce anger,
>   I will not again destroy Ephraim;
> for I am God and not man,
>   the Holy One in your midst,
>   and I will not come to destroy.

The God of covenant transcends the necessities of covenant agreement for the sake of the relation. While the promise cannot be understood apart from covenant blessing, it takes on a fresh meaning in the tradition of Hosea. The prophet accepts the limitations of the old form but handles it in a most creative way.

3. THE SUMMONS TO REPENTANCE

Among the forms employed by the prophets, the call to repentance does not occur often, but it is important for our understanding of the prophets.[37]

(1) The Form and Its Tradition

Of the several occurrences in Hosea the clearest is found in 10:12. The form, as it has been summarized by Wolff,[38] includes imperatives and/or prohibitions and often a deduction:

imperatives: Sow for yourselves righteousness,
                 reap the fruit of steadfast love;
                 break up your fallow ground,
deduction: for it is the time to seek the LORD,
                 that he may come and rain salvation upon you.[39]

The triad of imperatives is taken from agricultural images and is coupled with two of the great covenant words, righteousness and steadfast love. The deduction which follows is rather like the result of the suggested action. If the imperatives are heeded it will be a time of prosperity, i.e., covenant blessing. Westermann suggests that this form is closely related to the judgment speech. This is indicated in this passage, for the warning is followed by a parallel triad of indictments (10:13):

indictments:
    specific listing: You have plowed iniquity,
                      you have reaped injustice,
                      you have eaten the fruit of lies.
    general statement: Surely you have trusted in your
                      chariots and in the multitude
                      of your warriors.

As the second triad establishes the brokenness of covenant, so the first triad, which is our concern, is an appeal which can lead to restored covenant and the blessings that come through such restoration. Thus the form addresses itself to the possibility of restored covenant and places the responsibility for the restoration on the covenant people.

A second use of the form occurs in 12:6:

> imperatives: you, by the help of your God, return,
>   hold fast to love and justice,
>   wait continually for your God.

Though the word order is not as regular or as clear as in 10:12, the same triad of imperatives occurs. Again the imperatives are given objects, arranged in a telling sequence. The middle term, which is the one of stress, contains the two great covenant words, steadfast love and justice. The first and third members, which envelop the second line, name the deity as the object. The word order in the text forms a remarkable chiasmus which is not clear in the translation.

A third example of the form in Hosea is in 14:1-3, in which its use is somewhat more flexible:

> imperative: Return, O Israel, to the LORD your God,
> deduction: surely you have stumbled because of your
>   iniquity.
> imperatives: Take with you words
>   return to the LORD
>   say to him . . .

Twice in this form the object of the imperatives is Yahweh. This is a marked change from 12:6, where only the general term "God" was used. The deduction is not an anticipation of blessing to come as in 10:12 but rather is a reminiscence which serves as an additional indictment. The statement which follows is completely relaxed in form and we get a verbalization of repentance which probably is derived from a liturgic prototype.

The fourth use of the form is encased in a very complex passage in 6:1-6. The actual warning is perhaps not the work of the prophet but a use from liturgy to which he then attaches his own proclamation. In either case the form is evident:

> imperatives: Come,
>   let us return to the LORD;
> deduction: surely
>   he has torn, that he may heal us;
>   he has stricken, and he will bind us up . . .
> imperatives: Let us know,
>   let us press on to know the LORD . . .

The movement from the imperative to the cohortative does not reflect any significant variant in the form. It may provide a clue to the speaker but it does not lessen the force of the appeal. Again the name of Yahweh is twice invoked. The deduction is an interesting one, because it looks to the abrupt and decisive change in the situation from one of curse to one of blessing,[40] perhaps not unlike 10:12 which looks from drought to fertility in the imagery it employs.

Only after a quite different mood and form in verses 4-5 does the poem return to the warning form and this time with great power and force:

> Surely covenant loyalty I desire and not sacrifice,
>   knowledge of God, rather than whole offerings.

Here the form is handled quite freely. Instead of imperatives the strong preposition is used. In addition the impersonal tone gives way to a first person speech, no doubt to stress the urgency of the appeal. Thus the form is broken but the intent of the form is still readily apparent. The substance of this appeal in terms of steadfast love and knowledge is quite in keeping with the other appeals we have examined.

When we ask about the source from which this form is derived, there is a good deal of discussion and controversy among scholars on the question. H. W. Wolff,[41] following Erhard Gerstenberger,[42] has argued that the form is derived from wisdom traditions. As such it belongs originally in the context of the larger family unit and carries the weight of the family head (the father) as he gives norms and guidance for the well-being of the community. Thus the imperatives and prohibitions are the pronouncements of this authority figure. The deductions are simply the logical outcome of the rules for conduct. The urgency of the form is found in the assumption that the well-being of the community is at stake.

Wolff's argument is directed primarily toward Amos and the warnings there. Even if that is relevant for Amos, which is open to question,[43] it does not seem likely that it applies to Hosea. There is no argument at present that Hosea has close connections to the wisdom traditions. Rather his point of reference is consistently found in the old traditions of the covenant community. Thus even if the position of Wolff is sustained, the form is mediated to Hosea by another route. Even if the form is Wisdom in origin, in Hosea the most direct links are to be found with the traditions of covenant.

To be sure, the old covenant liturgies were not concerned with the restoration of a broken covenant. Rather they were designed to establish and ratify a covenant where none had existed. This means that the old liturgies do not call for return, do not appeal to Israel concerning a former position. Thus the function of "summons to repent" cannot be expected in those liturgies. Nevertheless the earlier covenant liturgies contain an element which does for them what the "summons-to-covenant" does in Hosea. The point of contact is a call to radical commitment, a demand that Israel stand up and be counted, that she cast off other gods and serve this one only, that she acknowledge this covenant God as central in her life and deny the power and relevance of other gods.[44] In Hosea the call away from the other gods is very closely linked to the call from broken covenant to true covenant. Again the form the prophet employs refers back to the liturgy of covenant. The summons to repent is, in mood form and purpose, derived from the demand for exclusive allegiance found in various liturgical forms.[45]

Among the more important of these early demands is the following:

imperative:	See, I have set before you this day life and good, death and evil. . . . therefore choose life,
deduction:	that you and your descendants may live (Deut. 30:15, 19).

The strong verb "choose" has here the same function as "return" in the prophets. It expresses the urgency and exclusiveness of the claim of Yahweh and the responsibility of Israel to make a decision about the covenant relation. The object "life" is a power-laden word which in the liturgy embraces the meaning of "righteousness," "covenant loyalty," "justice," and the other terms employed by the prophets. Moreover, the "deduction" corresponds to the one in the prophetic usage. Both the old liturgy and the prophetic summons confront Israel with the radical question of her existence and her destiny. Both affirm that to live outside the covenant relation is a decision for death.

A familiar parallel is that of Joshua 24:15:[46]

> imperative: *Choose* this day whom you will serve, whether the gods your fathers served in the region beyond the River,
> or the gods of the Amorites in whose land you dwell;
>
> deduction: but as for me and my house, we will serve the LORD.

Again in a context of liturgy and covenant making, with the strong verb "choose," the exclusive and radical claim of Yahweh upon Israel is asserted. In Deuteronomy 4:1-8 a like summons is given with the verb "heed" in verses 2, 6. This is the same term which stands at the center of the call to repentance in Hosea 12:6 and the claim of Deuteronomy 4:4:

> . . . but you who held fast to the LORD your God are all alive this day.

The call to repentance and renewal is the summons to cleave only to him.

In the very early summons of Exodus 19:5-6, the verbs "heed" and "hear" are both employed. Israel is defined as that people which listens and heeds. So the prophetic call to return is the call to reaffirm the covenant role of God's people. The form of prophetic speech again has its meaningful context in the liturgy of covenant.

(2) The Form and the Office[47]

From an analysis of Ezekiel 3:17; 33:1-9, H. Graf Reventlow has suggested that the role of "Watcher" was important in Israelite life.[48] Based on the function of the sentry who warned of the coming enemy and enabled the city to prepare, the image was taken over for covenant faith so that the watcher was one who warned of approaching doom and summoned the faithless to repent while there was still time. The approaching doom was known to be sent by Yahweh because Israel had disobeyed; i.e., it was the implementation of covenant curse. The watcher, informed by Yahweh, called Israel to return to Yahweh and live in covenant. There is convincing evidence that the prophet understood himself in this role in the life of the community (Isa. 21:6-7; Micah 7:4; Jer. 6:17; Hab. 2:1; Isa. 52:8; 56:10; 62:6). In this context the prophet has the responsibility of warning Israel that she has broken covenant and that punishment is sure to come (Hosea 9:7-8). However, punishment has not yet come and can be averted if Israel will genuinely repent.

The prophets must say two things which are difficult to hold together. Because Israel is guilty, they must declare that *punishment is certain*. But because Yahweh is sovereign, they must proclaim that *punishment may be averted*. Though the emphasis varies from time to time and from prophet to prophet, neither motif can be eliminated. As long as the prophets speak about a relationship which is dynamic and changing, one person can say both things. It is when the relationship is reduced to a system or theory that the fluidity of relationships is excluded. Too often the prophets have been subjected to rigid interpretations in which the ambiguity of relationship is not fully appreciated. Westermann in his criticism of Steuernagel rejects the notion that prophets are preachers of repentance.[49] But to say they do not perform this function is against the evidence.[50] The warning form indicates clearly that one function of the prophet was to summon Israel to repentance:

> "Be not like your fathers, to whom the former prophets cried out, 'Thus says the LORD of hosts, Return from your evil ways and from your evil deeds.' But they did not hear or heed me, says the LORD" (Zech. 1:4).

In the life of Israel the prophets embody God's recognition that the covenant has been broken, that brokenness must be punished, and that Yahweh is concerned to restore the perverted relation. Hosea's words take on fresh meaning when it is seen that he is not just against cult. He is concerned with the life (cf. Deut. 30:19) of Israel and the quality of her covenant relation. The words have urgency when heard in this context:

Sow for yourselves righteousness,
  reap the fruit of steadfast love;
  break up your fallow ground,
for it is the time to seek the LORD,
  that he may come and rain salvation upon you (10:12).

So you, by the help of your God, return,
  hold fast to love and justice,
  and wait continually for your God (12:6).

The prophet at times exercises the painful yet hopeful office of
summoning Israel back to covenant, the same covenant to which
Moses (Exod. 19:5-6) and Joshua (Joshua 24) demanded complete and immediate obedience.

The Forms in Their Context of Covenant

We may now suggest the function of the words and forms of the
prophetic tradition.

It has not been accidental that we have chosen the words "indictment," "sentence," and "summons" to describe the forms.
These terms accurately describe the intention of the prophet. The
oracles spoken are not spontaneous, random statements but are
delivered with great solemnity and significance. We are dealing
not with individual poems but with the technical language of the
courtroom. The context is a formal one. The hearers assume roles
in a trial situation. Here we want simply to call attention to the
terms which suggest this character. Among the more important of
these is the term "lawsuit," which in the RSV is, not very clearly,
translated "controversy."

Hear the word of the LORD, O people of Israel;
  for the LORD has a *lawsuit* with the inhabitants of the land (4:1).

Yet let no one contend,
  and let none accuse,
  for with you is my *lawsuit*, O priest (4:4).

The LORD has an *indictment* against Judah,
  and will punish Jacob according to his ways (12:2; cf. 2:2).

The context assumed by the prophetic oracles is a solemn assembly
in which Yahweh brings formal charges against his covenant part-

ner. In Hosea, this structure is made more specific because the trial proceedings are those of a divorce suit in which Yahweh brings suit against his faithless wife, Israel. The bulk of the material is a discussion of this charge, in which the evidence against Israel is shown to be overwhelming.

When the fickleness of wife-Israel is established, then it is clear that the marriage must be dissolved. The innocent party, Yahweh, is no longer burdened by a faithless relationship. This far the court scene carries us. But then Hosea departs from the script and from the courtroom to affirm that the betrayed lover, Yahweh, still wants the relation in spite of betrayal.

Other terms which support this judicial context include the call to hear, which is much like a bailiff announcing the beginning of court (4:1; 5:1); the act of bearing witness, "declare what is sure" (5:9); and the notion that evidence "answers" against the accused (5:5; 7:10). The context suggests that Israel is on trial for her life.

This, of course, does not mean there was an actual trial. Rather, the forms and words used by the prophet carry the connotations and make allusions to that kind of situation. The prophet may have dramatized this context to some extent; but even when he did not, the assumed context was clear both to speaker and listeners. Understanding the words in this context is important for reading between the lines and feeling the intention of the principals in the situation. In the trial situation the injured party, Yahweh, is offended and violated and eager to secure his rights. The accused, Israel, is hopelessly guilty as the evidence is ruthlessly presented. The prosecuting attorney, the prophet, represents the case of the plaintiff with vigor and competence. The outcome is never in doubt. Such gross crimes certainly mean the dissolution of the marriage and perhaps a death sentence upon the whore (see Deut. 22:22).

Taken as a dramatic situation, this form functions to stress the gravity of the situation, the indignation of the husband, and the fact that the relation has reached a point of no return. The question is simply: is Israel guilty as charged? If so, is the penalty divorce or death? Israel could scarcely miss the point if she is in any way sensitive to the intention of the drama.

And the drama, because it is covenantal drama, must always touch historical reality in some significant way. That Israel is on trial for her life does not mean simply that a "spiritual relation" is in jeopardy. Rather, we are talking about Israel as an historically, politically identifiable entity. The prophet and his people believed that the meaning of the drama would be implemented in history. Broken covenant means attitudes and actions which hinder the establishment of community. Death sentence means a disaster by which the historical effectiveness of this nation is destroyed. The issue in a very realistic way is life or death. The drama is in touch with both its legal foundations in the old covenant traditions and with the historical crisis of the present hour.

In our exploration of the basic forms employed by Hosea we have seen that the forms come from diverse sources. The judgment-speech (indictment and sentence) is a legal form which comes from a trial context in which the guilty party is charged with breaking an agreement and is placed under the appropriate penalty. The salvation oracle with its "I-speech" is perhaps cultic in origin, or perhaps behind that it derives from contexts of holy war. In any case it announces the decisive, perhaps unexpected intervention of Yahweh at a point of sore need. The warning speech may derive from wisdom teaching in which an authority figure guides the community in what is necessary for the good of the community.

However, that the forms come from a variety of places does not provide the primary clue to understanding their use in Hosea. I have argued that in each case the point of immediate reference for the prophet is not in the courtroom, nor the holy war crisis, nor wisdom circles. Each of these forms in one way or another has been taken into the covenant tradition of Israel. The judgment-speech now has as its point of reference the obligations of Israel to covenant. The indictment assumes a legal background which is found in the old covenant stipulations. The sentence assumes a list of clearly formulated penalties to be found in the covenant curses. Less directly the salvation-oracle is best understood by its reference back to the covenant blessings. And the warning-speech is closely related in form to the call to covenant and the paranesis in the older traditions. The forms are employed by the prophet not to make reference or appeal to the various places of origin, but to bring every aspect of his message into close connection with the older traditions of covenant.

By the time of the eighth-century prophets, it was apparent to those who really understood covenant that the essential dimension of the contemporary Yahweh-Israel covenant was its brokenness. Worship in this context was not the mere celebration of the covenant of the past but was concerned with the present condition of covenant, namely, its brokenness. This had several aspects. It was important to make the community *aware of brokenness*; to reiterate the *consequences of brokenness*; to *restore covenant*; and, if possible, to *prevent the awful punishment*. In the context of broken covenant the covenant liturgy, which had a political character from the beginning, becomes the setting for the great lawsuit which God brings against his people—Yahweh against his unfaithful lover. It is by the slight transformation of traditional forms that the fact of covenant is made into an event of covenant lawsuit. The assembly of public worship becomes the instrument whereby the drama of broken and renewed covenant is enacted.

It is in light of the covenant lawsuit that the function of the prophet can best be understood. He did not speak freely or lightly, but he spoke weighty words deeply rooted in a tradition of covenant. He did not speak indictments at random but in a formal way convicted Israel of her transgression of covenant law. He did not threaten freely or carelessly but reasserted the fixed formal curses upon the people of covenant. He did not call Israel away from worship to ethics but summoned Israel to a new radical decision for covenant which transformed both ethics and worship. He did not speak casually or merely optimistically of God's graciousness but affirmed that covenant has always been sustained by God's graciousness and not by Israel's obedience.

The prophet then has a formal and important function in the movement of Israel from broken covenant to renewed covenant. He may be understood as the spokesman for Yahweh, as the lawyer for the plaintiff, as the bearer of the covenant word to a people which tended to forget or deny covenant. In every part of his speaking, the prophet is informed and guided by the old liturgy which set before Israel her true calling. Apart from this calling of Israel, the prophet has no significance for Israel.

I am impressed with the way in which the tradition becomes a buoy for the prophet. The curse which he must proclaim is not *his own anger* but the consequence of brokenness. The indictment he must speak is not *his own disapproval* but the demands of Yahweh. The promises he extends to Israel are not *his own wishful thinking* but the assurances of Yahweh. The summons he speaks for a decision by Israel is not *his own sense of urgency* but the pressure of God's lawsuit with his people. The prophet speaks not for himself but for the covenant. See 2 Corinthians 4:5 for an analogy: the prophet preaches not himself but the covenant; Paul preaches not himself but Christ.

In much of our reading of the prophets we have read as though the prophet had no support or sustenance other than his own conviction and sense of call. And this in turn has produced an image of prophetic ministry which has left a man to his own inadequate resources. He has, it is commonly thought, nothing going for him except his own convictions and the force of his person. Unfortunately this sometimes leads to the proclamation of our anger, our disapproval, our wishful thinking, our own sense of urgency. Clearly the prophet is delivered from this hopeless exercise by a faithful appropriation of the tradition.

IV.

The Prophets and the Covenant Institution

Our concern is to determine the relation between the prophetic traditions of Hosea and the older historical and legal traditions of the Pentateuch. It has been widely assumed that the relation is at best remote and that we may speak in terms of discontinuity if not opposition between the two. However, the more recent study of the prophets requires new appreciation of the continuity between prophets and the old traditions and the shared theological intention of the two.[1] Thus far we have considered in detail two forms of evidence for the close relation. The first has been that the prophets grounded their work in the ancient *traditions of history and law* which are linked to the covenant memory of Israel. The second argument has been that the characteristic *forms* of prophetic speech were derived from and can be understood only in terms of the ancient liturgic situation in which covenant was made, remembered, and answered.

In this chapter we suggest a third line of argument for the relation of the prophets to this old tradition. This argument comes as an answer to this kind of question: If the prophets knew the old traditions and used them so well and if the prophets normally cast their speech in the language and forms of the old covenant, where in the life of the covenant community did the prophets find their appropriate *place of speech*? Though the answer is complex and fraught with great difficulty, the answer we will here suggest is increasingly given by scholars: the men who knew the covenant traditions so well and who employed the covenant forms so effectively most likely had their place in the institution of covenant, namely, as *speakers in the cult where the liturgy served to remem-*

91

ber and renew covenant. It is to be stressed at the outset that this third evidence of continuity is much more precarious than the last two and obviously is not offered here as a final statement on the question.[2] But it is equally certain that any serious attempt to understand the prophets must not a priori dismiss this possibility.

The Usual View Concerning Prophets and Cult

Current scholarship has moved a great distance away from the view of the prophets which is normally assumed in the church. Indeed, we are in danger of making the older view into an unfair caricature when we discuss it. However, without attempting to caricature it, it is important that we contrast that view with the approach that now seems more acceptable to scholars.

The factors which led to the view which has been propagated in the churches and the seminaries are not difficult to uncover. The conventional view has been dominated by an evolutionary assumption about the history of Israel.[3] It was widely held that biblical faith progressed from the pre-Mosaic period of patriarchal religion to the fulfillment of the faith in Jesus Christ. This approach emanated from nineteenth-century German scholarship under the influence of Hegel. Charles Darwin applied the evolutionary hypothesis to the biological sciences and Herbert Spencer to history generally. When applied to the history of Israel, history was viewed as "progressive." Naïve forms gave way to more mature and sophisticated forms. Folk religion was replaced by individual religion. Cult religion was supplanted by ethical religion. Polytheism gave way to monotheism. In each case the newer phenomenon was superior to the preceding form, because (as the hypothesis) that is the way history moved.

Unfortunately this view of the prophets is still alive in many circles. The prophets are seen as the most significant advance on the way from the patriarchs to Jesus. They represent the greatest single departure from the religion of Moses and the most significant preparation for the Christian event many centuries later. Thus in Amos we have the appearance of *ethics* in Israel's faith. Ethical religion stands in contrast to the Pentateuchal religion of "cult and magic." In Jeremiah and Ezekiel the emergence of *individualism* was an innovation which discarded the community religion of the early traditions. Finally, in Second Isaiah full-blown *monotheism* appears, which supersedes the polytheism of the early religion of Israel.

This hypothesis led to radical and erroneous assumptions concerning the prophets. It required the judgment that the prophets had no significant relation to the old traditions but had evolved from them and were really new and different. Stress was put on the discontinuity between the prophets and the old traditions. The prophets are not understood in terms of the covenantal-cultic traditions but *in opposition* to them. At every important point (ethics, monotheism, individualism) the prophets combated the more primitive, unreflective orientation of the earlier period of history. A study of the Torah does not help at all in understanding the prophets. Rather, the Torah speaks of a quite different religion, from which Israel has finally emerged. The prophets then are the real witnesses to the authentic faith of Israel. What came before is something other than mature Old Testament faith and can be safely ignored.[4]

A second assumption which has controlled our understanding of the prophets is philosophical individualism, which stresses the free spirit and genius of the individual. This notion, which had appeared already in the Renaissance, came to full expression in the European Enlightenment in the eighteenth century. Often without our knowing it, this assumption has been a most important factor in our approach to Scripture. The important persons are those uninhibited by society and unshackled by conventional norms and standards. Indeed, this view of individual freedom was incorporated into the general evolutionary assumption outlined above: individual religion is superior to folk religion. This view was imposed upon the prophets and served to tear them out of the context of community in which they lived. Thus it was no longer possible to think of the prophet as a member of a community, but he must be seen in opposition to his community. And in terms of the written materials of the prophet, it follows that these ecstatic utterances were completely free form, quite detached from any institutional form of expression. This assumption deprived the prophet of his proper historical context as a member of a believing community in the Near East for whom life was largely circumscribed by the orders of society. Instead he became a European of the Romanticist tradition without relation to his community. Again, a quite alien assumption is imposed upon the prophetic tradition.

A third factor which contributed to this misunderstanding of the prophet was the tendency of Reformation thought of the sixteenth and seventeenth centuries to employ a verbal shorthand which equated Old Testament with Law and New Testament with Gospel. Perhaps this is a fair procedure in broad theological discussions, but it is certainly unsound if one takes seriously what the Biblical materials really say. To dismiss the Old Testament as "law" suggested that there is nothing in the traditions of either the Pentateuch or the prophets except endless commands and prohibitions which leave men condemned and powerless. When the term "law" was applied to the Torah (Pentateuch), this completely ignored the great narrative sections which testify to the great Gospel-deeds of Yahweh. When applied to the prophets, it suggested that the prophets were critics of society who scolded and condemned. This terminology of "law" is still alive in the church. It leads to a disregard for the real power and fullness of Old Testament faith generally and the prophets in particular. This general misunderstanding has resulted in the Old Testament's being a closed book for Christians. The prophets are summoned into play only on "Social Action Sundays." Much of our approach to the Old Testament has been careless and irresponsible, with inarticulated interpretive principles of a very narrow kind. It will not do any longer to dismiss the Old Testament as *Law* and let it function only in contrast to New Testament faith.[5]

Finally, among the influences we will suggest for the widespread misunderstanding of the prophets is that of a Protestant bias against institutional forms of religion. Every establishment which leads to cultic practice is regarded as an expression of superstition and magic which denies the power of the Gospel. Thus in its crudest form we have assumed that a fully Protestant faith is a body of ethical teaching which is devoid of liturgic dimensions:

> To worship rightly is to love each other,
> Each smile a hymn, each kindly deed a prayer.[6]

Given the support of the evolutionist approach, the prophets then are the great Protestant teachers of an ethical religion. One of their primary functions is to attack the cult and all corporate expressions of the faith. They introduce authentic "Biblical" faith which rejects and refutes what the old traditions had offered in an earlier period.[7]

From a variety of sources the common view of prophets in the Protestant tradition has offered a picture of men who stood outside and opposed to the system, for the system is evil, per se. Protestants then could picture themselves as the successors of "men-against-the-system." The notion of "prophetic preaching" has come to mean a general impassioned attack on everything organized and established. From this perspective, it is difficult to set the prophets in the context of the covenant institution of cult.[8]

The Cult and Israelite Faith

Our discussion of the prophet in the covenant institution of cult suggests the need for a new understanding of the nature of the prophet. But the prior need is for a fresh approach to the institution of cult. Mowinckel has defined cult as:

> "the visible form, fixed and ordered by the community, through which the religious (pious) experience and the fellowship between 'deity' and 'community'—the connection with the divine and his honor—take place, that is, have their beginning, come to expression and reach their goal."[9]

One cannot object to the definition, but it is too broad to be useful. It is necessary to define the term explicitly in terms of Israel's covenant faith. Thus we may say that cult is the public assembly in which Israel did and said what needed to be said and done to implement the covenant with Yahweh in every dimension of her life. The combination of New Testament polemics against Judaism, Protestant bias against corporate worship, and the evolutionistic contrast of ethics and cult have led to a misunderstanding if not hostility toward the public worship of ancient Israel. It has too often been assumed that the center of Israelite liturgy was in the offering of sacrifice and the "magical" acts which are linked to the flow of blood and the giving of oracles, apparently in rather esoteric and superstitious ways. Whereas the prophets are men set apart from this action, the cult itself has been regarded as a copy of the Canaanite ritual which is interested in fertility and which functioned by manipulation of deities which are subpersonal. Obviously one shrinks from thinking of the Old Testament prophets in this context!

It is clear that there are many parallels between the worship of Israel and the rites of Canaan. Much borrowing has taken place, and to deny this would be to treat the evidence lightly.[10] However, having granted this, it must be firmly insisted that sacrifice, blood, magic, are not the center of the worship of Israel. While Israel had these in common with her neighbors, these elements do not define her worship.[11] To properly understand the worship of Israel we must investigate not what she shared with Canaan but what was distinct in her worship, for it is in this distinctiveness that the center of her faith is to be found. The cult of Israel is to be distinctly characterized as worship in which the Deity speaks and Israel listens and answers.[12] The entire covenant liturgy which we have outlined in our first chapter is a liturgy of speaking and hearing. The word of the Deity is his recital of saving deeds and his new demands upon his covenant people. The answering word of Israel is a word of faith and obedience, of hearing and heeding. Thus the familiar call of Deuteronomy 6:4 is structurally at the center of covenant worship: "Hear, O Israel." Indeed, Israel is Israel only as she hears. When she stops listening, she ceases to be Israel.

The entire liturgy of covenant is a genuine dialogue which defines the proper relation between the two parties to covenant. Yahweh is Yahweh precisely because he is the speaking God whose very word determines the destiny of Israel. And Israel is completely a creature of his speaking, living by his word and having no other support or purpose in life than the faithful hearing and effective response to that word (Deut. 8:3). To be sure, there are sacrifices and festivals of many kinds which Israel appropriated from a non-covenantal tradition of worship. But where Israel is genuinely Israel, the pagan assimilations are subsumed under and made to be vehicles for this worship of Word and answer. Thus the sacrifices of feeding the deity and appeasing him are transformed by Israel's covenant for Israel's worship. They are now rites of communion and solidarity. The festivals which had fertility as their concern are transformed into great affirmations of the deeds of this God with his people. The question of the assimilated elements is not, "Did they borrow it?" but rather, "In what way does it edify the covenant relation of speaking and answering?"[13]

In Israel as nowhere else in the ancient East, worshipers had to do with a person—not a reactor to be manipulated, not an agent to be exploited, not a power to be deceived, but a person with whom honest and deep relation is both possible and necessary. And because he is person, this means the relation is never secure. It is always fluid and changing. Never predictable but always precarious and alive. Never static but always fresh and explosive. Never stationary but always mobile and open. Because Yahweh is this kind of person, the cult which is involved with him must also be a form of worship which is changing, precarious, alive, fresh, explosive, mobile, and open.[14] Any other cult denies Yahweh, whom Israel knew to be working in her history. Thus the issue in understanding the worship of Israel is simply, did her cult adequately allow for the kind of relation Yahweh willed with Israel?

It is in this context that a cult centered in the dialogue of Word and answer is both meaningful and essential. The covenant liturgy of address and response is Israel's best attempt to come to terms with this God who invaded the life of Israel. It is in speaking and answering more than in any other activity that a vital relation is possible. The liturgy of the Word when put in its institutional form is the liturgy of covenant, for covenant is the continuing expression of relation-in-dialogue. Israelite cult then is not, as has often been suggested, something prior to, in opposition to, or a perversion of covenant. Rather, it is the essential vehicle of covenant. It provides the situation in which the speaking-answering of covenant comes to specific and formal expression. The cult exists for the sake of the covenant. It derives its modes of operation and its purpose from the covenant relation which is nourished by and dependent upon periodic dialogue in an institutional form.

We are now prepared to understand the so-called prophetic polemics against cult (e.g., Hosea 6:6; Amos 5:21-27; Isa. 1:10-15; Micah 6:6-8; Jer. 7).[15] These are not, as careful study will show, protests against Israel's involvement in worship, but against worship which had ceased to edify covenant, against rites which did not serve the dialogue of Word and answer, against a liturgy which did not function as a legitimate vehicle for relation between the speaker of the Word and the creature of the Word. The cult the prophets denounced had ceased to be a genuinely Israelite form of worship. It had been perverted. Now it served to manipulate, appease, and exploit the Deity; i.e., it failed to take seriously who Yahweh was in the life of Israel. But the prophetic polemic is not against Israelite covenantal worship. It is against the temptation of Israel to escape the relation and void the covenant, the temptation which was always alive in the worship of Israel. But the protest calls Israel back to a form of public worship in which the liturgy gives the covenant relation of dialogue meaningful expression in the life of Israel.[16]

The Prophet and the Covenant Word

When we have correctly understood covenant faith as a dialogue between the Word of Yahweh and the answering word of Israel, we can better understand the function of the prophet as the mediator of covenant between Yahweh and Israel.

It is primarily as *mediator* that the role of the prophet is to be understood, as the one who stands between the two covenant parties to enable them to relate to each other. From this it follows that the prophetic role and function is to be understood primarily as a continuation of the *role and function of Moses*[17] in the early history of Israel.[18] The function of Moses was to enable Israel to live in covenant with Yahweh, which means: to proclaim Yahweh's mighty deeds in the past; to declare Yahweh's stipulations for Israel; to hear Israel's solemn oath of allegiance; and to pronounce over Israel the blessings of faithful covenant and the curses of broken covenant (see chapter I).[19]

In the line of Moses, Joshua, and Samuel, the prophets speak the covenant word and evoke a faithful response from Israel. They are to be understood as the true heirs of Moses who do in succeeding generations what Moses did for his generation, namely, bring Israel into existence as a faithful covenant community.[20]

The fact of covenant in Israel's life is not a "spiritual idea" but a relation embodied in institutional forms. From this it follows that the role and function of the prophet is in some way linked to this institutional form, the cult.[21] The prophet is not one who speaks as a disconnected individual without social, historical, or institutional context. Thus we must speak not simply of the person of the prophet but also of the *office*[22] of the prophet, to which he is ordained by the community and in which he is expected to function as speaker for Yahweh to Israel and as speaker for Israel to Yahweh. This does not mean that the factors of ecstacy, inspiration, and personal experience are denied or eliminated. But it does mean that these factors now are to be understood in terms of the needs of the community and the institutional ways in which these needs are met. Yahweh's call to one to be a prophet is a call to be a responsible leader in the community of faith.[23]

The prophet, as an official ordained to speak the word for Yahweh, is not free to speak just any word that comes into his head. Rather, he speaks with authority the word which Yahweh addresses to the community of faith. Or to say it another way, the word the prophet speaks is a covenant word, intended to serve the covenant relationship. As such, his words are heard as the words of the covenant Lord.[24] The words of the prophet, in the service of the covenant, depend upon the situation of the covenant in his day. (1) When the covenant has been broken but the patient concern of Yahweh is still seeking, he admonishes repentance, summoning Israel back to covenant. Hence, the oracular form of repentance. (2) When the covenant is broken and the anger of Yahweh has been provoked, he offers evidence that the covenant has been broken (indictment) and declares the punishment to come (sentence). (3) When Yahweh continues his gracious concern for Israel in spite of broken covenant, the prophet announces grace (promise). Each of the major forms of prophetic speech fits the office of covenant mediator. Each shows that his real subject-case is the condition of the covenant, or, if we may put it in modern language, the status of the church as servant of the Word.

Now having said that right cult in Israel is *a vehicle for the covenant word* and having said that the prophetic role is the *bearer of the covenant word,* we may go beyond the explicit evidence to face the question: Where did this officer of covenant most likely function? The most plausible answer is in the cult of the covenant. The liturgy made it possible for the ordained officer to speak the words which have been transmitted as prophetic words. The established religion of Israel included instruments of criticism and renewal, agents of reform and repentance, so that prophets may be seen as a central part of the life of the community of faith. If we have rightly defined cult, it is not necessary to assume that the prophet must stand outside of it or oppose it. Because this cult sought to faithfully reflect the covenant relation, by definition it included this dimension of covenant worship. Israel at worship had to face up to who Yahweh really is, in all his sovereign freedom. When the prophet is understood as the bearer of the covenant word in the institution of covenant worship, we can understand why he spoke in traditional forms and why he alludes so frequently to the old historical and legal traditions. These are the forms and traditions relevant to the community in which and for which he ministers. Because he is nurtured in this heritage and called to serve the community, he could not think or speak apart from the conventional uses of the community. The prophetic tradition as we have it is in the normal, rather fixed form that it is because it reflects the controls and conventions of public worship. This does not mean that the prophet did not have freedom.[25] But he most often expressed his freedom, not in violation of form, but in the creative use of the normal forms.

In this context we may better appreciate the so-called polemics against cult, of which Hosea 6:6 is a most familiar one:

> For I desire steadfast love and not sacrifice,
>   the knowledge of God, rather than burnt offerings.[26]

It is clear that the prophet is not against cult and for ethics. He is for orientation of the community to covenant in every dimension of life, including both ethics and cult. The prophet never divides up life as we are inclined to do but deals with every dimension of it in relation to the graciousness and summons of covenant. Thus to interpret such an oracle as anti-cult is to avoid the radicalness of the claim the word makes upon the covenant people. Yahweh who created Israel for his own now calls his people to change in a most radical way. He calls Israel to be his people even in the present circumstance. The prophetic office in Israel's liturgy is the instrument of his speaking.

In this connection we may note the problem presented for Israel both by false cult and by false prophet. The concern for false cult, as we have shown, is not that it is cult but that it is cult which does not express covenant.

Earlier in our discussion concerning Canaanite assimilation, I suggested that Israelite distinctiveness is found in new words, new intentions, and a different world-view because of faith in a different God. "True cult" is found in Israel wherever the intentions of covenant are real and authentic. Covenant with Yahweh is grounded in a distinctive world-view. This world-view holds that life is whole and joyous when there is perfect obedience to Yahweh's purpose for justice and peace. Israel's worship is legitimate when it expresses those dimensions of covenant.

It is "false cult" whenever these intentions and world-view are not operative, and this is what the prophets condemn. False cult is found when Israel goes through the motions of covenant but does not intend covenant. Such false worship is characterized by: the assumption that the worshiper leaves the sanctuary just as he came, without being changed in any way; liturgy which avoids all decision-making and responsibility; a preoccupation with the worshiper's well-being; a disregard for the purposes of the covenant Lord; the assumption that this is our worship and we are answerable to no one; and, therefore, worship which permits and sustains "business as usual." Worship which has no integral relation to the covenant by which it is measured is false worship. It is worship which has forsaken the political-secular-historical-social idiom and has reverted to the religious idiom of Israel's neighbors.

Concerning false prophets, it is not necessary to assume that they are prophets linked to cult.[27] Rather they are prophets, either associated with the cult or not, who do not speak words within the context of covenant. As the liturgy, so the prophet is judged by his fidelity to the covenant. The words of the true prophet are grounded in and informed by the covenant. He brings the Lordship of Yahweh to bear upon every dimension of contemporary life. He witnesses to Yahweh's mighty deeds, to stress the utter graciousness of Yahweh and the total dependence of Israel. And this is scandalous, for Israel in her well-being would rather assume that she had achieved what she has. The true prophet speaks the covenant stipulations for the present day and witnesses to the total claim of Yahweh upon his people. Out of the blessing and curse tradition he affirms that Israel is answerable to Yahweh for her existence. He speaks to Israel to proclaim that Yahweh in his utter graciousness and radical Lordship must be faced by Israel. He will not go away, and Israel cannot ignore him. The true prophet does for his people in his time what Moses did for Israel in an earlier time.

There is agony in speaking of Yahweh's graciousness and his sovereignty, for this of necessity calls into question Israel's self-seeking investments. So there also appeared in Israel the temptation to compromise the radicalness of the covenant. The false prophet, who did not articulate the full impact of the covenant, spoke words not so hard to hear. He presented to Israel a covenant which Israel could have on its own terms. He spoke as though Israel is not answerable. Even if Israel does not honor covenant stipulations, she can have covenant blessings (peace) (Jer. 6:14; 8:11). The promise, " 'Peace, peace,' when there is no peace," means to promise blessings when Yahweh will not give them. The false prophet assures Israel that there are no curses to come even though covenant-breakers will be punished (Jer. 14:13-16). He talks about history as though Yahweh were not in charge and therefore as though Israel were not held accountable (Jer. 28). It is often said that the false prophet tells people what they want to hear. This may be true, but the real issue lies deeper. The question at stake is the control of history. The true prophet is one who calls Israel to face Yahweh's purposes for justice and peace even when these purposes clash with our own apparent best interests. The true prophet knows Yahweh is in charge and calls Israel to face that fact. The false prophet, through a variety of compromises, lets Israel think her own purposes count most and that Yahweh can be appeased, manipulated, influenced, bought off, to work Israel's will. The Lord-servant relation is perverted so that Israel becomes master of the relationship.

While there are many passages dealing with the question of false prophecy, Deuteronomy 13:1-5 is the clearest on the point we are making. The false prophet is one who turns Israel away from Yahweh. The alternative is to:

> walk after the LORD your God and fear him, and keep his commandments and obey his voice, and . . . serve him and cleave to him (vs. 4).

This admonition contains the classical terms of covenant. The false prophet is one who suggests to Israel that she can have life on a basis other than covenant.

The clearest example of the separation of life from covenant obedience is in Ezekiel 13. Each of the four units gives one mark of the false prophet: verses 2-9, they speak from their own hearts, without any word from Yahweh, with reference to nothing beyond themselves; verses 10-16, they promise peace for the covenant-violators, which denies the Lordship of Yahweh (cf. Jer. 6:14; 8:11); verses 17-21, they use magic to manipulate their lives and so deny the Lordship of Yahweh (see Deut. 18:9-14); and verses 22-23, they have not called Israel to repentance as covenant demands (see Ezek. 33:1-9).

To be sure, this criterion is general and not well defined. In any given situation it is ambiguous and difficult to apply. Other criteria might be more precise, but they tend to be simplistic and inadequate to express the full meaning of the covenant.[28] Thus in a given situation—e.g., Jeremiah 28—the prophet is left to agonize and it is not clear who is false and who is true. The prophet himself may doubt and wonder, to say nothing of the community. But he has no real appeal other than to the tradition of covenant. When we ask, by whom or what is he judged to be true or false, the answer is the total tradition which appeals to Moses and the liturgy of covenant and the body of teaching which has clustered about the figure of Moses.

The same criterion is applied to both dimensions of Israel's life. False cult and false prophets are false because they are not in the service of covenant. True cult and true prophets accept the responsibility to speak of the Lordship of Yahweh and the relevance of covenant to all of life. Both agents of Yahweh, cult and prophet, face great temptations to compromise. They have in common the difficult task of mediating covenant. Indeed, they are inextricably bound together in nurturing and disciplining Israel to live faithfully as Yahweh's covenant people.

The Prophets and the Faith of Israel

Though we cannot recover the precise words or deeds of Moses with any degree of accuracy, it is legitimate to assume that the Pentateuch as we now have it preserves an authentic memory of the faith from the time of Moses.[29] This refers especially to the covenant tradition of Exodus 19-24 and the liturgic and legal materials of the tradition of Deuteronomy. These together suggest the understanding of life and history which was normative for Israel, a view of life and history which celebrated the Lordship of Yahweh and the servanthood of Israel. Or put another way, life was viewed in terms of this relationship of covenant. Worship was designed to maintain and upbuild this relationship.

Worship, which stood at the center of the early history of Israel, was primarily concerned with covenant. In the Sinai and Deuteronomy narratives, Moses is remembered as the one who mediated covenant for Israel. Moreover, from such passages as Deuteronomy 5 and 31:9-13, we are led to believe that the covenant traditions were intended as liturgies and were used repeatedly in periodic festivals so that the covenant might be restored, renewed, reasserted, updated; and this use preserved the vigor and relevance of the original. Thus the traditions feature a constant retelling of the mighty deeds, a giving of new laws for new situations, and, to a lesser degree, the taking of covenant vows and reciting of blessings and curses.[30] Worship characteristically dealt with the important task of keeping the covenant in repair in order to preserve the faith and character of Israel as a community of faith. In the midst of many historical crises when the true character of Israel was sorely tried, the covenant liturgy served to maintain and restore it.

Allowing for differences in mode and circumstance, our study brings us to the conclusion that in their own time in very different circumstances, Hosea and other prophets like him continued the work of covenant mediation. For their time and situation, they did precisely what Moses did. Whereas Moses dealt with the problem of establishing the covenant and creating a community of the covenant word, the prophets faced the problem of restoring the covenant and thereby re-creating or renewing the community of the covenant, which for a variety of reasons and under varied pressures nearly disappeared.

Thus the continuity of the prophets with the traditions of the Torah sheds new light upon the prophets, upon the Torah, and upon the nature of God's people as the creature of the Word. In every generation in countless historical crises, the problem is to reassert in effective ways what it means to be God's people, to assert in new ways the deepness of God's grace revealed in his saving deeds, to announce with new power the claim of God upon his people through the law. The challenge is to be the faithful watchman, to proclaim with urgency the summons to repent and return, to help the community see that she always stands before life and death, blessing and curse. To be God's people, she must find meaningful ways of choosing life and blessing.

V.

Hosea as Bearer of the Word

Having given a general analysis of the relation of the prophetic office to the problems of covenant faith, we need to face the question raised by a concern for the person of the prophet. If we say that the prophet is ordained to an office, what then happens to his personality and the authenticating factors of inspiration and ecstasy which have been so stressed in prophetic study? That is, if the prophet is understood in terms of his office, are the prophets all alike? Are they simply carbon copies of each other?[1] Here we consider this acute problem by looking more closely at Hosea.

Hosea: Person and Office

The characteristic approach to the prophets has been to emphasize the greatness of the individual, the loneliness of his encounter with Yahweh, his isolation from community, and the fact that his message has been forged out of deep personal crises of suffering and of wrestling with the purposes of Yahweh.[2] This has been a part of the general assumption that personal religious experience was more advanced and mature than community religion. Now, having called that assumption into question, we are tempted to go to the other extreme. In a mood which takes the community seriously and appreciates the importance and validity of institutions, we are in danger of losing the man completely in our quest for the office. This would suggest that we can't really know anything of the man, and if we could, it would not be important, because we are interested only in his functioning as an official of the covenant community.

Our concern here is to show that one may fully accept the notion of prophet as officeholder without surrendering the distinctness of each prophet as a person. While the prophet functioned in an official capacity, each man had the freedom and responsibility to do so according to his own inclinations and experience. The prophet necessarily worked and spoke in light of his personality and his experience. As he functioned as a prophet, he did not cease to be the man he had become. While it is most plausible that some of the great prophets of the pre-exilic period served officially as covenant-mediators,[3] they would not all do it in exactly the same way. They would not make precisely the same emphases. They would not select the same images and figures for effective communication. The way in which a man fulfilled his role as mediator would be determined by the kind of man he was.[4] Parallels are not hard to find. In the established traditions of Protestantism, particularly those which have some well-defined order for worship, the character and inclination of the priest or minister will very much determine how his ministry is executed and the word proclaimed, even though his work is circumscribed in an official kind of way.[5] If we are to understand properly the tradition of Hosea or any other prophet, we must pursue the study of his person, his life, his historical context, his molding experiences. Though what has been preserved is cast in traditional and perhaps cultic language, still we must press the quest for the prophet involved in the history of his time. Our characterization of cult in the preceding discussion shows that involvement in cult and in history are not mutually exclusive. The historical experience of the man gives his work its uniqueness. The cultic responsibility compels a fairly fixed form of expression. The important point is that uniqueness and conventional formulation are not antithetical to each other.

Hosea serves as an excellent example of the point. Only a man who has had the deep painful personal experience of the prophet could have executed his prophetic ministry in the form in which Hosea did. It is not conceivable that an Amos or a Micah could have felt so passionately or suffered so deeply, that an Isaiah could have been aware of the radical dimensions of broken and renewed covenant. It is first of all in Hosea that the covenant crisis of Israel is viewed as a divorce proceeding in which the violated husband brings charges against his faithless wife (4:1-3). It is only in this context that every dimension of life may be viewed as a form of harlotry (4:10-14; 5:4-7; 6:10; 9:1-3). Economics, politics, cult, and judicial proceedings are seen as evidence for a violated marriage vow. Only one who has experienced this kind of humiliation can indict Israel as a people which cherishes harlotry (4:10), as infected with a spirit of harlotry (4:12), so that they cannot return (5:4).[6] The revulsion and disdain he feels, the scorn alternating with mortification, are the tones of a man who has trusted boldly and been betrayed, who has loved deeply and been abandoned. This kind of man knew the agony of God saying:

> What shall I do with you, O Ephraim?
> What shall I do with you, O Judah? (6:4).

> How can I give you up, O Ephraim!
>   How can I hand you over, O Israel!
> How can I make you like Admah!
>   How can I treat you like Zeboiim? (11:8).

He knew the desolation of being forgotten (8:14; 13:6).

But the man who has suffered most deeply and most innocently is also the man who most clearly knows the power of costly redemption. This is the faith of a giant of a sufferer, a man who had been through it, loving the unlovely, pursuing one who seemed not to want him, trusting himself to the untrustworthy. Such a man makes the most radical indictment upon Israel. In such a context he affirms that the problems are not moral and cultic but theological, i.e., covenantal. But alongside this he can make the most radical affirmation of grace:

> I will not execute my fierce anger,
>   I will not again destroy Ephraim;
> for I am God and not man,
>   the Holy One in your midst,
>   and I will not come to destroy (11:9).

Hosea finds fresh dimensions in covenant. He finds the strength to break out of the confined explanations of his contemporaries and to assert the radical *non sequitur* upon which Israel's faith had been built from the beginning:

"I have seen the affliction of my people who are in Egypt, and have heard their cry because of their taskmasters; I know their sufferings, and I have come down to deliver them out of the hand of the Egyptians, and to bring them up out of that land . . ." (Exod. 3:7-8).

". . . the LORD your God has chosen you to be a people for his own possession, out of all the peoples that are on the face of the earth. It was not because you were more in number than any other people that the LORD set his love upon you and chose you, for you were the fewest of all peoples; but it is because the LORD loves you, and is keeping the oath which he swore to your fathers . . ." (Deut. 7:6-8).

It is important that Hosea is here not introducing a totally new element into the faith of Israel. His personal experience and his moment in history permitted and required him to enter deeply into the faith of his people. This dimension of Yahweh's graciousness for Israel which Hosea stresses had been there from the beginning. Indeed, Israel's existence as a historical entity was dependent upon it. But Hosea is equipped by time and circumstance to express this traditional element in fresh and emphatic ways. Interestingly, the clearest expressions of this motif are in the Northern traditions. This supports the thesis of Wolff reported above.

We have suggested that Hosea occupied an office. He knew the past. He cherished the tradition. But because of his own personal history, he knew in fresh ways what the faith was about. Thus, in the office such a man finds power to speak the saving word to Israel, the word about her existence and destiny. This word affirms that she is a creature of covenant, that she has no other claim or hope, that her life can be safely entrusted to this incredible God about whom Israel sang:

> He does not deal with us according to our sins,
>   nor requite us according to our iniquities (Ps. 103:10).[8]

A man in an office! Israel assembled and heard words she had heard often before. But the word borne by the faithful servant took on new power, new validity, for it was a word spoken by one whose life authenticated the word. Such a man is made into a prophet when the word claims him as the word claimed Hosea.

The covenant community is transformed when it assembles and hears the word mediated by such a man in such an office. The community of faith judged him authentic, as attested by the preservation and transmission of his tradition. When a man stands before the community and speaks the word he has heard, we cannot distinguish the man and the office. To deny either is to miss the awesomeness and power of the moment of proclamation when the live word of God is spoken by the covenant mediator in the covenant assembly.

Something happened in Israel through this man who suffered and trusted. It was not primarily an event in the life of Hosea, or in the life of Gomer, or in the relation between them. It was rather Yahweh's way of dealing with his people, his way of reorienting history, of reclaiming his partner, of reasserting his sovereignty and remaking the "church" for himself. Then and now, the way he works is by persons of faith ordained as bearers of his word to his people who live to answer his word.

Hosea 2:2-23: Covenant Broken and Restored

We will consider this unit[9] in detail to illustrate the way in which the conventional (official) and unique (personal) elements are brought together. This unit is selected because the form stands out with clarity and because a variety of traditional motifs are employed. Moreover, the conventional language is turned in a way which surely reflects the distinctive orientation of this particular man.

1. VERSES 2-13: BROKEN COVENANT

These verses are certainly to be regarded as a unit. It is concerned with a single characteristically prophetic point; namely, to show that the covenant has been broken and to voice the consequences of infidelity. The beginning in verse 2 shows that the forms employed are legal, with the use of the term contend ("plead"), which suggests a trial situation.[10] The verse contains three elements: (a) the call to trial, which simply names the defendant and repeats the imperative; (b) the charge introduced by a strong preposition, "surely":[11]

> Surely she is not my wife,
> and I am not her husband—

i.e., the covenant has been dissolved because of infidelity; and (c) the hint that the woman may save the relationship if she completely changes her ways. This provides the setting for what follows. Thus verses 2-13 are about broken covenant. That is completely conventional. But the fact of brokenness receives a certain expression as befits this particular covenant spokesman.

In what follows, three forms are utilized:

(a) The indictment which gives evidence for Israel's guilt:

vss. 4-5	*surely* they are children of harlotry.
	Surely their mother has played the harlot;
	she that conceived them has acted shamefully.
	Surely she said, 'I will go after my lovers . . .'
vs. 8	*And she,* she did not know that it was I
	who gave her the grain, the wine, and the oil,
	who lavished upon her silver and gold which
	they used for Baal.
vs. 13	. . . the feast days of the Baals
	when she burned incense to them
	and decked herself with her ring and jewelry,
	and went after her lovers,
	and forgot me, says the LORD.

These indictments call for little comment. We have already noted that harlotry is rooted in the old legal traditions as a covenant violation. The first indictment concentrates on this theme. The second applies the theme to fertility. The third becomes more specific with reference to cultic practices and culminates with the powerful "forgot me," which ties it to the traditions of Deuteronomy. Each of the charges is linked to "going after other gods," which obviously contradicts the first commandment of the decalogue and of the *Shema* (Deut. 6:4).[12]

Concerning formal elements, the first group is introduced with a series of three recurring "surely," the second with an emphatic personal pronoun, and the third ends with an inverted word order, "me they forgot!" Thus the form and the link to the old legal traditions make it certain that the indictment will be recognized and taken seriously.

b) The threats which give the consequences of broken covenant:

vs. 3   *lest*[13] I strip her naked
     and make her as in the day she was born,
and make her like a wilderness,
     and set her like a parched land,
     and slay her with thirst.

vs. 6   *Therefore* I will hedge up her way with thorns;
     and I will build a wall against her,
     so that she cannot find her paths.

vss. 9-13a   *Therefore* I will take back
     my grain in its time,
     and my wine in its season;
and I will take away my wool and my flax,
     which were to cover her nakedness.
Now I will uncover her lewdness
     in the sight of her lovers,
     and no one shall rescue her out of my hand.
And I will put an end to all her mirth,
     her feasts, her new moons, her sabbaths,
     and all her appointed feasts.
And I will lay waste her vines and her fig trees,
     of which she said,
"These are my hire,
     which my lovers have given me."
I will make them a forest,
     and the beasts of the field shall devour them.
And I will punish her . . .

The result of broken covenant is the inversion of all prosperity and well-being so that death results. The first of these threats is rooted in the historical tradition of the Exodus and sojourn in the wilderness when Israel was so utterly helpless and dependent upon Yahweh (see Ezek. 16:4-8).[14] The coming of thorns and thistles is a conventional threat against those who live in an agricultural context.[15] The taking away of produce upon which Israel relies is in accord with the covenant curses and may refer to seizure by the enemy (Lev. 26:16; Deut. 28:38-41) or failure to produce (Lev. 26:20). The end of cultic feasting is perhaps foreseen in Leviticus 26:30, and the coming of wild beasts is a familiar curse (Lev. 26:22). The threat of humiliation by nakedness is pervasive. It refers to exile, which is spoken of in Deuteronomy 28:48:

> ". . . therefore you shall serve your enemies whom the LORD will send against you, in hunger and thirst, in nakedness, and in want of all things . . ."

To be sure the particular language of "lovers" shows the hand of the prophet, but the materials are closely linked to the traditional curse language.

The formal element which dominates the sequence is "therefore," which links the threat to the indictment. We may note also "and now" in verse 10 which adds urgency to the oracle. The first person verb with Yahweh as subject is most characteristic and is widely used here. Again, this is in keeping with the older curse formulae.

(c) The summons to turn back to covenant:

> vs. 2b that she *put away* her harlotry from her face,
>   and her adultery from between her breasts . . .
> vs. 7 She shall pursue her lovers,
>   but not overtake them;
>   and she shall seek them,
>   but shall not find them.
>   Then she shall say, "I will go
>   and return to my first husband,
>   for it was better with me then than now."

Rather unexpectedly there is the hint by the prophet that the threat may be averted if Israel will turn back and honor her covenant with Yahweh. Clearly the total unit does not anticipate this. But there is a faint hope for the impossible. As we have suggested, the summons to return is rooted in the old traditions. The verb "put away" in verse 2 is the same verb used in Joshua 24:14 when Israel is admonished to serve Yahweh only.[16] The second of these, verse 7, has the characteristic word "turn" and is not unlike 6:1 and 14:1-3, which speak of repentance in the language of the cult.[17] In 14:1-3 there is again a rejection of other gods, which draws it into the sphere of the old commandments which insist on the exclusive worship of Yahweh. Again, in this form, the prophet stands in the old tradition.

Thus in this unit which employs the forms of indictment, threat, and admonition, the prophet makes use both of older forms and of older traditions[18] to describe the brokenness of the covenant in a lawsuit formulation.

2. VERSES 14-15: THE POSSIBILITY OF NEW COVENANT

In these verses, following the indictment of verse 13 we anticipate a more radical threat. And this expectation is reinforced by the "therefore" with which verse 14 begins. However, the form is employed in an unexpected way. It no longer dwells on the consequences of broken covenant. It affirms that Yahweh is acting in a new and decisive way so that covenant may be restored. The formal elements do not take us very far. They include the "therefore," now the third in the sequence, and "behold," which marks a decisive intervention of Yahweh. Most important for form is the use of four verbs with Yahweh in the first person which are really the substance of the unit:

> I will allure her . . .
> I will bring her . . .
> I will speak to her . . .
> I will give her . . .

The four statements show that what is to come is not derived from Israel's status but from the freedom of Yahweh, who acts as he chooses. It is this arbitrariness upon which Israel's faith is based:

> I have seen the affliction of my people . . .
> [I] have heard their cry . . .
> [Surely] I know their sufferings . . .
> I have come down to deliver them out of the hand of the
>   Egyptians (Exod. 3:7-8).

> . . . I will make of you a great nation . . .
> I will bless you . . .
> [I will] make your name great . . .
> I will bless those who bless you . . .
>   him who curses you I will curse (Gen. 12:2-3).

The two beginning points of Israel's faith are rooted in this arbitrary, radical action of Yahweh. All else is derived from his sovereign declaration. This way of speaking is rooted in the early traditions.[19]

Content supports this judgment on the form. The traditions of wilderness sojourn and finally the Exodus itself are cited as the ways in which the new decisive deed of God may be understood. The act is utterly new, and after verses 2-13 is quite unexpected. But its newness stands in close connection to the old forms and traditions.[20] Only in such a context can the point really be grasped. It is always at her moment of despair that Yahweh comes to Israel, even in her moment of covenant breaking and infidelity.

3. VERSES 16-23: THE REALIZATION OF NEW COVENANT

What had only been promised in verses 14-15 is now proclaimed with clarity. The unit is difficult to handle because the various motifs make it appear rather fragmentary and disorganized. However, the unit of the passage may be discerned on two lines of evidence: (a) the basic promises correspond to the threats in verses 2-13 and (b) the various motifs are all concerned with the restored covenant, even though they seem to deal with quite diverse matters.

The correlations with verses 2-13 suggest that we have the precise inversion of broken covenant, i.e., restored covenant. (a) Verses 16-17 are concerned with the Yahweh-Baal conflict which clearly is at the center of the preceding trial scene. (b) Whereas Yahweh is forgotten in verse 13, in verse 17 it is Baal who will no longer be remembered. (c) In verse 2, Israel is compelled to remove her harlotry, while in verse 17 Yahweh will remove the cause of harlotry.[21] (d) Verse 18a is concerned with the restoration of covenant in its "natural creation" aspects, which has no exact parallel in the preceding, but we may note that the threats of verses 9-12 really speak of "un-creation," the cessation of the pattern Israel can depend on for growth and reproduction. If we correctly assume that Hosea is using the language of fertility religion, then the mention of grain, wine, and oil obviously has much broader implications. It has to do with creation as a covenant blessing which is taken away from the unfaithful. Yahweh's curse is to interrupt the sequence for which he has been reliable (cf.

Gen. 8:22 and Hosea 4:3). In verse 18a, creation is restored
because of Yahweh's faithfulness.[22]

(e) The promise of security in verse 18b[23] corresponds to the
allusions to distress and humiliation in verse 10. The general
promise of peace recalls, of course, the covenant blessing (Lev.
26:5-6) which is related to the absence of the wild animals threatened in Hosea 2:12. This may also relate to the covenant with the
beasts of the field just considered (Hosea 2:18), because Yahweh's
covenant with them permits Israel to lie down in safety.

(f) The marriage motif is resumed in verses 19-20. The relation
is now "for ever," the direct antithesis of verse 2 where the relation is dissolved. (g) The great covenant words which follow stand
in sharp contrast to "harlotry," "shame," and "lovers." (h) The
reference to "knowing Yahweh" in verse 20 is the answer to verse
8, in which the harlot Israel did not know Yahweh as the giver of
her life.

(i) The fertility imagery of verses 21-23 clearly relates to the
end of fertility in verses 9-13a. It may be that the verb "answer"
here is related to the mention of "season" in verse 9, for the words
have the same Hebrew root. In verse 9 the agents of fertility do not
answer at the time when they should. In the restored program of
verses 21-22, they answer on schedule because Yahweh guarantees it.[24] That which he has taken away in judgment, he now
gives in graciousness. The answer motif is important if this unit
reflects the dialogue of liturgy. Begrich has shown that the com-
plaint or lament often receives an answer which gives assurance
of being heard by God.[25] In this passage, the answer of verses
21-22 is addressed to the situation of despair announced in verses
9-13. Note also in verse 15, "answer" refers to a restored covenant
relationship. (j) Finally in verse 23 the covenant formula is reasserted, which controverts the divorce formula of verse 2.

Not only do the motifs of verses 18-23 correspond to the preceding unit, but they also hold together in terms of new covenant.
The themes we have suggested are (a) restored marriage as over
against harlotry, (b) a friendly, orderly "creation" as over against
one which destroys (cf. vs. 12), (c) the giving of peace, the end
of exile, invasion, and hostility, (d) the resumption of the blessings

of growth, fertility, and reproduction, and (e) the reassertion of the covenant formula.[26] These may be reduced to three, for (a) marriage and (e) covenant formula both speak of relation, and (b) orderly creation and (d) resumption of fertility are both concerned with the material side of the relation. Thus we have assurances of a *renewed* relation (a, e) which promises *prosperity* (b, d) in the realm of nature and *security* (c) in terms of history; i.e., a covenant which gives blessing in every dimension of life, just as the unit of verses 2-13 promised trouble in every phase of Israel's life.[27]

Whereas verses 2-13 had spoken the curses over Israel, verses 16-23 speak of the blessings which had long been recited in the covenant liturgy. The formal marks would seem to support this with the threefold "in that day," which refers to the day when the covenant is fully realized. The movement of the unit may be roughly related to the liturgic piece in Deuteronomy 30:15-20 in which Israel is offered life and death. Verses 2-13 are an account of the way Israel chose death. Verses 16-23 are an invitation to choose life and a delineation of what this means.[28]

It is clear that verses 2-23 may well be regarded as a unit. It does not really matter if a later hand has combined the words of the prophet from various periods. The unity is still cogent. But it is not at all necessary to divide these sections as though they belonged to different periods. Nor is it necessary to regard the latter part of the unit as being from a later hand. The formal as well as the dramatic unity of the whole is apparent. The movement of thought is from the recognition of broken covenant and the execution of curse to the gift of the new covenant and the bestowal of blessing. In between, verses 14-15 are the call to Israel to return to Yahweh. This suggests that Israel's transition from death to life depends solely upon Yahweh. Yet to receive this profound gift, Israel must again enter covenant.

When our study of the unit pays attention to form and tradition, we come to the possible, though not necessary, conclusion that we do not have here a series of small units which were later brought together but rather a whole which dramatically brings Israel from utter estrangement to the assurance of restored relation. In such an interpretation each part of the whole serves an important function. To tear the sections apart is to deny the power which each has when it stands with its other parts.

In terms of our understanding of the office of the prophet, we may ask finally about the setting of this unit. If the prophet refers so much to the old historical and covenantal memories, if he employs the forms of the covenant, each of which may be rooted in the old liturgy, where did he most likely speak these words? The answer to which we are driven: he spoke these words in a solemn assembly when Israel gathered to renew the covenant with Yahweh which she had so flagrantly violated. He spoke them at the moment of covenant-making in the cultic assembly. We may suggest that this occurred at some critical moment in the life of Israel, perhaps at a turning point in the Syro-Ephraimite war, or if he lived so long, in connection with the final siege of Samaria after 725 B.C.[29] But that is beside the point. We are concerned to stress that Hosea 2:2-23 is a covenant form, which is well suited to use in a variety of situations, whenever Israel earnestly wished to restore the covenant she had broken.

4. THEMES STRESSED IN THE ORACLE

While the unit is fairly conventional in its construction and development, we may note the themes which mark it in a distinctive way. The first of these is the imagery of sex and marriage in which Yahweh is described as the faithful husband, Israel as the faithless wife, and the gods of the nations as the lovers who cooperate with the harlot. The motif of "lovers" (vss. 5, 7, 10, 12, 13) is a powerful one, expressing both the cultic unfaithfulness as Israel worshiped Baal (4:12-14) and political intrigue in which Israel paid tribute money to foreign powers (see 7:8-11).

The perceptiveness of the prophet is obvious as he employs this figure. The theme permits the prophet to penetrate the covenant crisis in a way that Amos and even Isaiah could not do. Hosea does not concern himself in the same way with the conduct of Israel but is concerned with the attitudes and motivations which stand behind the conduct.

The other notable image of the unit is fertility. Though it is known elsewhere, Hosea uses it more consistently than any other tradition. It is remarkable that the prophet who so values the sojourn tradition is also the one who speaks most contemporaneously in the language of fertility religion; i.e., he speaks in terms of the most urgent problem of his time.[30]

Our analysis of 2:2-23 has demonstrated the use of much conventional form and tradition. Now we point out that it is the creative use of these particular motifs and themes which reveals the forceful and creative personality of Hosea. It is one thing to announce that covenant is broken. It is quite another to speak in terms of sex and broken marriage vows, and to see political involvement as gifts from lovers. This subtle use of image cannot be explained by reference to the tradition because the use Hosea makes of the imagery has no clear antecedent. We can only conclude that it was the person of the prophet who made a particular use of the tradition and thereby made it relevant and urgent for his time and circumstance. The reasons he did so are close at hand. One is his personal experience of marriage and betrayal in which he learned what brokenness and graciousness are all about. Second, no doubt because of his own experience, he had the courage and insight to express the faith in terms for his own time, in the language of the very syncretism he wanted most to combat.[31]

The same prophet who consistently employs the *traditional forms* and refers to the *memories* of his people is the one in whose words the pathos of his *person* shows through. Hosea refuses to choose between the traditional and the personal. I find it not at all implausible that the office of covenant mediator in ancient Israel would be occupied precisely by this kind of creative person who in his own experience had understood what the covenant was about. But at the same time, his own experience was illuminated by that very tradition in which he lived and which he regarded as so urgent for his people.

Prophet, Tradition, and Crisis

The covenant faith of Israel persistently came to its most vigorous and eloquent expression in the times of political and cultural crisis. It was a faith which emerged out of the crisis of the Exodus and received creative reformulation precisely when it had to respond to situations in which its validity and relevance were called into question. Thus we may describe the creative moments of Israel's faith as those times when tradition was engaged with crisis.

By the tradition, we mean the shared memories of Israel's past, that body of shared data out of which Israel lived which was expressed in fairly fixed forms. It is important for our analysis to note that the tradition by which Israel lived consists not only in a normative content but no less in characteristic forms in which the content is expressed.

By crisis we refer to a situation in the community when the old faith no longer seemed adequate or relevant. This would come about for a variety of reasons.[32] It may result from entrance into a new culture context, such as the entrance into Canaan with its own alternate religious traditions. It may result from internal political pressures in which the conventional forms of power no longer can cope with the situation, as in the period after Samuel. It may arise because of the threats from the outside for which the community seems to have no adequate response, as in the Assyrian-Babylonian periods. It may be expressed in terms of a people who are linked in self-understanding to the land, and who need a new way of speaking when they have been separated from the land, as in the Exile. Or it may come when the community is concerned for its purity and is set in a situation where many apparently unclean elements threaten, as in the period of the restoration under Ezra. We suggest simply that the peak moments of Israel's history in the Old Testament are times when the traditional expressions and forms of the faith are called into question by unprecedented situations.

The work of Hosea can best be understood as one of those confrontations between tradition and crisis in which something creative happens. Most of our discussion has been concerned with the delineation of the tradition out of which Hosea spoke. It affirmed that Yahweh was Lord of all of life, that Israel must serve and trust him in all of life. The crisis of the time, so well described by the historians, was caused (a) by the problem of religious syncretism in which Yahwism was subtly merged with the fertility religion of Canaan, whereby God became a force to be manipulated, and (b) by the threat of the Assyrian armies.[33] The question posed to the tradition by the crisis was simply this: Can this blind uncompromising faith in Yahweh and allegiance to him protect us in this time of crisis? Those who accepted the tradition said "yes." Those who saw the crisis from a different perspective were not so sure. But it remained for someone to engage these factors with each other. This is precisely what Hosea did. As he brought tradition and crisis together, both were changed. The tradition was changed so that now as never before it was understood profoundly under the imagery of sex and fertility. The crisis was changed because now it was no longer a question of survival and well-being but a question of faith and covenant-keeping.

The piece on covenant renewal in 2:2-23 illustrates the point. In verses 2-13, the crisis is carefully considered. The prophet speaks especially of the involvement of Israel in Canaanite worship. The judgment pronounced speaks of the end of cult, the devastation of agriculture, nakedness and "being uncovered." This no doubt alludes to the Assyrian pressures which became so acute in 735 B.C. and the years following. But the prophet does not simply speak about the crisis. He sets it in the context of the tradition, so that very ordinary things like religious syncretism and international politics are related to Yahweh's sovereign purposes. By this way of speaking, the ordinary historical circumstances are presented as a radical crisis in covenant.

The passages which speak of the possibility (vss. 14-15) and realization (vss. 16-23) of covenant say yet another thing about the crisis. They presumably address the situation when Israel can see that all is lost. She is in despair and knows that her way of life (cultural assimilation and international gamesmanship) has led to defeat and death. But the prophet does not simply speak about the terrible state of affairs. By recourse to the tradition, he is able to say something different about the crisis, which is not apparent in the situation itself. He is able to say that what seems to be a situation of despair is a situation in which the covenant God can give his blessing and restore the relation.

Now if the crisis addressed must be an historical one, then

verses 2-13 could not apply to the same crisis as verses 14-23, for the one assumes a judgment to come, the other assumes that it has happened.[34] But the crisis faced by people and prophet can well be presented in the liturgy so that the same assembly may experience both the threat over its life and the promise of something new in the midst of despair. This is not unlike much liturgy which can embrace the mood of remorse for sin and the great joy which comes from dedication to new obedience.[35] This does not mean that cult is remote from history, but only that liturgy gives Israel a view of history in its broader dimensions from which the Lordship of Yahweh cannot be eliminated. In the moment of the liturgy, then, Hosea 2:2-23 witnesses to the whole historical period of Hosea, from the invasion of Tiglath-pileser in 743 B.C. down to the fall in 721 B.C., with a hope of history yet to come. And in this recital about his time, the prophet relates it to the faith which Israel confessed for generations but had such difficulty in actualizing.

The prophet has the responsibility of engaging tradition and crisis in a responsible way. The methodology by which scholars have proceeded has generally stressed the crisis but not the tradition. This means that the conventional analysis of the prophet has been concerned with the history of the period, with the personality of the prophet and the way in which this person viewed this history. In a reaction against this, tradition critics have been much concerned with the form and substance of the tradition, at times to the neglect of the crisis. This approach runs the danger of minimizing the person of the prophet, the pressures he faced, and the problem he addressed. It tends to suggest, no doubt unintentionally, that there is nothing creative or unique about this particular formulation by the prophet. Our analysis suggests then that in approaching the prophets we need more balance in a study which takes full account both of the tradition out of which he speaks and the crisis to which he addresses himself and in which he must live.

The prophet insists that the crisis must be taken seriously and cannot be ignored. He insists with equal urgency that the tradition of the community is relevant if we rightly understand and interpret it. The theological point is that the covenant Yahweh made with Israel is effective in any kind of circumstance. Speaking this word about Yahweh's Lordship over Israel makes it most plausible that he had an official function in the cult. Cult may be regarded as the place and action whereby the tradition is brought to bear in creative ways upon the crisis of the time. It is the achievement of the prophet that he makes a connection between crisis and tradition. This work clearly requires a creative person.

VI.

Prophetic Ministry in Our Own Situation

An understanding of prophetic ministry in Israel will not make our own responsibility and opportunity for prophetic ministry any easier and perhaps not much clearer. But it may protect us from false assumptions which create unnecessary problems in discerning our ministry. The foregoing discussion relieves us from several popular notions which are burdensome and immobilizing today. (1) The prophet in Israel or today is not called to invent a new message. We are not called to say something never said before or to do something never done before. To be sure, we are called to be imaginative and creative, but we do not have to create something out of whole cloth. (2) Our call to be "charismatic" about a prophetic ministry does not require us to operate outside the office to which we have been ordained. There is a widespread notion that the two are incompatible and we must choose between them. The wedge between "prophetic" and "priestly" or "pastoral" roles is both false to Biblical faith and an impossible burden. It is worth noting that the greatest of the prophets, Jeremiah, also most clearly exercises the priestly function of intercession.[1] (3) The one who exercises a prophetic ministry is not to set out all alone with his private faith and the force of his personality. We have the great resources of the tradition, and we have the support of a community which has gone before and is yet to come (see Heb. 12:1). (4) Because of the power and relevance of the tradition, the prophet is not turned loose with his own feelings, either of anger so that he must "tell people off" or of wishful thinking so that he may "promise the sky" to the community of faith. We have standing ground in something more lasting and authoritative than our own

124

hopes and needs for success. Our ministry is grounded in something outside ourselves so that we are freed from undue anxiety about our accomplishments.[2] (5) Perhaps it hardly need be said, but it follows also that the prophet is not one who must guess about the future actions of God. The prophet is not one who predicts but one who discerns the characteristic ways of God's history in the past and so also in the future. This gives us some assurances about the future without the pressure to have to know precisely what is coming next. (6) The prophet, in his office and as a person, embodies the covenant which he mediates to God's people. This means we have more than words with which to work, though words are not unimportant. We also have ourselves, our bodies, our presence. Our call and our office require that we pay attention not only to what we say but also to what we do. This does not mean that we offer ourselves as paragons of moral virtue but rather that our actions be investments of ourselves as the sign of God's investment in the history of his people. The prophets of Israel understood well that actions often speak louder than words, and so they acted when their words were no longer heard. The contemporary counterpart of that may be our prophetic involvement in the economic, social, and racial conflicts of the day. Not only our mouths but our "warm bodies" may be the mediation of covenant.[3]

Our Ministry Between Tradition and Crisis

We have characterized tradition as the whole body of memories which have to do with God's gracious, sovereign deeds with his people. Crisis is the new situation in which the old traditions in their conventional forms and formulations are inadequate or obsolete. The prophet has the urgent task of handling the tradition in ways which address it relevantly to the new crisis situation.

Standing in the tradition of the faith of Moses, we may cite several examples of prophets who engaged in this task. Hosea is a prime example. He called men to see the new situation for what it really was in eighth-century Israel. To some the crisis must have appeared to be a threat on the part of the Assyrian army, complicated by the weak monarchy of Israel. The prophet speaks to show

Israel that the situation is not what it seems to be. It is not a time
dominated by Assyria and the facts of political weakness. Rather,
it is a time when Israel has violated covenant in every dimension of
life and now Yahweh is acting to reassert his sovereignty over
his wayward people. To *rightly discern the crisis* is necessary before
appropriate response can be made to the new situation. If Israel
thought the problem was Assyria, then one kind of response was
called for. If in fact the problem was with Yahweh and not Assyria,
then a quite different response was indicated.

In the eighth century, because men were frightened by Assyria
and despairing about the political situation, there was no doubt a
widespread feeling that the old traditions of Yahweh's covenant
could hardly help now. After all, Tiglath-pileser III is not the
Pharaoh of the Exodus. There is now no Moses, no Joshua, no
David. In these times we are more nearly left to our own resources.
The old helps are not available. The old urgency is now spent and
we live in a time when nothing important is going on. The old demands of Torah can be safely ignored in the new situation as we
worry more about survival and public security.

Against this the prophet must reassert the Lordship of Yahweh
over Israel's history. He must show again that any king not responsible to the covenant will be an ineffective one (8:4-6). He must
assert that a foreign policy which tries to ignore the demands of
Yahweh is doomed to failure (7:8-13). He must make clear again
that violation of the public good leads to public misery (6:11b—
7:7). Even in this situation *the old traditions are valid*. It is still
true that health and security are found in Yahweh. It is still
true that adherence to his stipulations is the way to social well-
being. It is still true that Israel's role in history is in reference to
Yahweh's gracious purposes. Clearly the validity of the old traditions for the present depends on a correct appraisal of the situation. When the present crisis is read as an Assyrian threat, the old
traditions don't count. But when the present crisis is shown to be a
crisis in covenant, then the old traditions are still valid.

If the new situation be rightly discerned in terms of the old traditions, then the prophet has one other task: he must set down the
options and *compel Israel to choose*. He does not make the choice

for Israel. That she must do for herself. But he must make it clear that the situation in light of the crisis requires a choice. And even not to choose is to make a choice. He must set the issue and show the consequences so that the choice in the present is seen as a choice between life and death. Thus the choice may lead to the "rain of salvation" (10:12). The choice involves an embrace of justice (12:6). The choice requires a decision about armaments and foreign policy. Either Israel will trust in alliances, or in arms, or in Yahweh and his purposes (14:3). The decision which takes this specific form is really a decision to be Israel or not to be Israel in the present time. To be Israel is to choose life, which means justice, wholeness, security, freedom, responsibility.[4] To refuse to be Israel is to choose death, which means continued corruption, wickedness, insecurity, false alliances, and false securities which will lead to destruction and historical annihilation. And then the prophet leaves Israel to face the issue. No one can face it for her.

In another time another prophet has the same responsibility. In the sixth-century exile, Second Isaiah must help Israel *discern the new situation*. In exile under the Babylonians, Israel despaired. She was sure Yahweh had forgotten and betrayed her (Isa. 49:14). The situation was dominated, according to the despairing exiles, by Babylonian power and ruthlessness and by the failure of the whole Jerusalem establishment. The latter also meant the failure of the covenant. But the prophet makes a quite different discernment of the situation. He asserts that God's word of commitment is alive even now (40:8), that his promise is still in effect (55:3), and that the word is now to be expressed in the rise of Persia under Cyrus (45:1). To his people the situation looked like a struggle between Babylon and Persia, with Israel losing either way. To the prophet the events of history are laden with meaning and this meaning has to do with the present involvement of Yahweh in the situation. With this premise the situation looks quite different.[5]

He must *insist that the old traditions count even now*. Surely in exile it was clear that the old traditions were bankrupt, that the promises of Yahweh were now empty and hopeless. The central message of the prophet is the assertion that these traditions still have power and all of history is informed by them. So he declares that Exodus (Isa. 43:1-7) is still a characteristic way for Yahweh to act.[6] Even the promises to Noah have power for the present (54:9). As Yahweh has manifested his power before all the gods in the old days, so even now this tradition erupts in the present so that his power and control as well as his concern for Israel are apparent for all to see. Even in exile Israel may trust the God in whom our fathers trusted. And anyone who thinks Yahweh has now quit on the tradition understands neither the vitality of the tradition nor the present circumstance.

Having stated that the present moment brings the old traditions to fruition, the prophet must *call Israel to make a decision*. It is possible either to act as though Yahweh is not in charge of history or to affirm his Lordship. One is a decision to stay in exile. The other is a willingness to go home, even if led by a despised Gentile (45:9-13). Israel must make a decision. Either she trusts in Yahweh's liberating word or she does not (55:6-11). One is a decision to stay in exile. The other is the risk of going home. Obviously the decision is based on how one discerns the present and trusts the traditions. But the prophet can only set the issue. Then Israel must make the choice for herself.

In another time when the old traditions seemed remote, Jesus has approximately the same function.[7] He must help his people Israel *discern the real situation*. To some it must have looked as though the Roman Empire was the central fact of history and there was no relief in sight. Or the legalistic extreme of Jewish piety was so rigorous and firmly entrenched that to many the possibility for acceptance and therefore wholeness was most remote. But Jesus insists that this is scarcely a correct reading of the situation. He sees something else. The present is the time of the kingdom, and this means that neither Rome nor legalism is the central fact we must face. The real issue in the present situation is the kingdom about which men must make a decision (Mark 1:14-15).[8]

Jesus then insists that the old tradition is not voided but is still valid.[9] As in the Exile, many must have thought that surely God had now forgotten his people and we must make other arrangements. But Jesus obviously believes that the old traditions are most relevant for the new situation of the kingdom. Indeed, the whole event of kingdom makes sense only in the context of the tradition. So he affirms the completion of the Torah (Matt. 5:17-20; cf. 19:17; 22:34-40).[10] Indeed his claim for what the present demands is stated in Mosaic-prophetic categories (Matt. 23:23).[11] The continual allusion to Old Testament texts and the preoccupation with Torah and temple indicate the devotion of Jesus and the early church to the tradition.[12] The tradition is indispensable for the announcement of the new situation in the New Testament.

Because the new situation must be proclaimed, the people of God must decide how they will receive it. Jesus calls men to make a choice, to accept or to reject (Matt. 6:24). Thus he uses the word "repent" (Mark 1:15), the same word used by Hosea (12:6; 14:1-2) and Second Isaiah (55:6-9). And Jesus, as the others, makes it clear that this is a choice for life or for death. Again the choice will be made on how the present is discerned[13] (whether it is the moment of the kingdom or the time of the Romans) and how the tradition is regarded (as still relevant or not). But the covenant mediator can only set the choice and explore the consequences. Then the people are left with the choice (John 6:67-69).

These parallels are instructive when we come to think of the prophetic ministry of our own time. A prophetic ministry is imperative and difficult whenever the situation is so new and different that the old traditions no longer supply clear guidance and adequate motivation for facing history responsibly. Whether Assyrian threat and Canaanite syncretism (the problem faced by Hosea), or Babylonian exile and syncretism (the situation in which Second Isaiah worked), or Roman power and Jewish legalism (the context of Jesus' career), the times required a prophet. We now have a similar setting for our prophetic ministry, a moment when the old traditions mechanically applied seem no longer to give clear guidance or supply adequate motivation for facing history responsibly. The dimensions of this crisis are numerous:

(1) Respect for authority in every phase of life is on the wane.

This is true in every social group; in church as well as state, in families as well as educational institutions.

In the civil community we attempt to deal with this crisis with a passion for "law and order." But as Sydney Harris has observed,[14] the adherents of law and order are most often more concerned for order than for law. "Law" has within it the notion of justice and even of change, whereas "order" most often means to keep things "our way" without attention to the equity of the situation. Robert Theobald, in commenting on the authority crisis of our time, concludes that

> . . . we are teaching young people to respect authority at a time when authority is no longer possible, and when we ought to be struggling together to understand the world in which we live. We still say to them, *listen and learn*, rather than *strive with us*.[15]

The authority crisis in our time is certain and deep. Because this crisis, like every crisis, threatens us, we are tempted to be firm and pretend it has not happened. This no doubt is a false discernment of the situation.

(2) We still seek to live by an economic theory and with emotional investments on economics which are informed by a situation of scarcity. The central problem of that situation was survival. But now with our affluence, the problem is not at all survival economically, but rather responsibility before the many options we face because of our prosperity. John Galbraith[16] has perceptively shown that the real economic question of the new time is not survival or security but the relation of private interests and public good. Again the crisis is not faced simply by reaffirming the old ideology.

(3) People refuse to stay in "their places." In domestic situations this results in racial disorders. On the international scene, this means the rejection of everything that hints of colonialism.

(4) Automation and cybernation have taken jobs from people and the time-honored alliance between job and worth is called into question. A by-product is the use of leisure, which in an older day had appeared by definition to be evil.

(5) Confusion between public and private areas of responsibility creates anxiety. Now it is argued on some fronts that sexual

behavior no longer is subject to public supervision. This attitude toward sexual behavior is most popularly championed by *Playboy Magazine*. Concerning that reading of the crisis, the issue is not whether we should have sexual freedom or not (we obviously do) but whether we image ourselves as autonomous agents who can do what we want or whether we are participating members of a responsible society. The specific issue is insignificant unless it is set in the context of the larger question. It is ironic that those who read the crisis against "sexual freedom" most often are also those who lack a clear understanding of the person-community issue which is at stake. Conversely, it is now held that poverty is no longer the responsibility of the person or family but is now a responsibility of the public sector. It becomes increasingly difficult to distinguish what is "mine" and what is "ours."

(6) Adherence to national causes and policies is no longer the neat, clear matter it seemed to be. On the one hand the claims of the world community call for a new definition of patriotism and on the other hand such things as "selective conscientious objection" call into question the whole assumption about the claims of state upon the individual citizen.

(7) The advances in medicine and biochemistry make the ultimate questions of life and death much more complex. Who supervises the decision for birth in a world where babies had been planned and selected? And what of the population explosion? And who is responsible for sustaining life in a person who has been reduced to vegetable status or for ending that life?

(8) The moral and technical problems related to the military syndrome now are so remote from us that they seem almost to be out of control so that no responsibility can be exercised over them. Have they become a new demon in our world or is there an option?

(9) The knowledge explosion means that education cannot hope to transmit as it has in the past the knowledge needed in any given field. Then what are the norms for education and who has responsibility?

(10) The whole matter of urbanization, with industrialization, poverty, impersonalization, mobility, anonymity, and the increas-

ing urban ghetto, has called into being a new kind of existence
which makes little sense and which clearly seems beyond our control. Harvey Cox has of course placed a positive value on the urban
phenomenon. But that is not his great contribution. More important, he has called attention to the fact of urbanization as a theological crisis about which we have some fresh homework to do.
It is no longer possible to view metropolis in conventional ways
which much conventional theology has sustained. Now the question
must be reworked if we are to recognize the new situation of crisis
in its true dimensions.

(11) A variety of art forms and expressions in our time seem
to reject all classical meanings and offer in their place a celebration of chaos.

We could extend the list indefinitely. But this will suffice to support the claim that we are called to live in a new situation.

The prophet has the task of helping the people of God to rightly
discern the new situation. What really are we witnessing before our
very eyes? A quite popular view among "believers" is that we are
now in a situation where the faith of our fathers is quite irrelevant.
And indeed the faith of the fathers is not relevant or valid when
it is understood in a mechanical, literal, external fashion. When
we read the new situation, it is possible to conclude that the world
is "going to the dogs," that all the old values are being destroyed
with nothing to replace them. All the values we have learned to
honor and maintain are now being swept away by persons and
forces who have no responsible sense of history. Many things are
being threatened. Our idyllic notions of right and wrong, "a place
for everything and everything in its place," "the good old days,"
"the American way of life," "law and order," the capitalist ethic,
worth measured by productivity, "being good," "my nation right
or wrong"—all these are in danger of being lost. Those who discern the present situation in this way claim that we must act to
preserve the old values. They recommend, for example, tighter
laws on flag-burning to maintain nationalism, tighter restrictions on
housing to guarantee small islands of "our kind," the prayer amendment to keep our schools "Christian," a proposed constitutional
amendment to keep state legislatures oriented to rural values and

interests. Clearly most of these actions, whether justified or not, are motivated by loyalty if not nostalgia for the past and a fear or panic about the loss of such values. If it is assumed that the God we worship is in some unique way to be identified with these values, then "religious motivations" also drive us to an attempt to save the old order.

But is this a correct discernment of the present situation? The prophet has a task to expose false discernments, of which the above are, in my judgment, clear examples. The prophet has the responsibility to discern the present as a place where the forces of the fully human community may be coming to expression. "Law and order" is often an attempt to suppress the legitimate claims of people to be human. The "Communist conspiracy" may be in fact a vigorous attempt by the disenfranchised and disinherited to share in their legitimate human heritage. Pluralization and secularization of society may be breaking the bonds of parochialism and sectarianism which have prevented people from the exercise of free choice and genuine responsibility for their own humanity. Cybernation may be a gift by which persons discover that joy and meaning come from being fully human and not from holding a job. To properly discern the present situation is to suggest that the forces which are new in our time may be movements toward the full humanization of society, and that fearful efforts to hold on to the old order may in fact be resistance to humanization because humanization threatens some of our vested interests—economic, political, social, psychological, or theological.

The crisis this poses for Biblical faith is pretty well expressed in the move of the church from the farm to the metropolis. In the more parochial, homogeneous situation of rural life, Biblical faith was a more obvious option. Being close to the soil, close to family and community, made moral and ethical questions comparatively simple. Social relations were less complex, and the dependence of the human community upon its natural environment made such things as worship, prayer, faith, more reasonable options. But the transfer of "church people" to metropolitan areas where men can manage their environment with relative ease, where help apparently comes not from God but from a variety of social

agencies, faith seems not such an attractive option. It is by no
means clear that the God of the farm is any longer relevant or
necessary in a fully urbanized situation. The formulations and
institutional structures of that rural faith are not relevant. They
have evolved out of an agrarian context and cannot be transplanted.
And because that formulation of faith seems not to be relevant,
"believers" apparently have two options. (a) To work desperately
to hold on to the old order or (b) to face the crisis without the
faith because is is irrelevant.[17] The task of the prophet is to make
clear that this is not a correct reading of the situation. In fact,
the new situation is an invitation for the world to become human;
and wherever humanness can emerge, there Biblical faith is coming
to expression.[18]

The second task of the prophet is to make clear in what ways
the old traditions are still valid in the new situation. This, of course,
depends upon rightly discerning the new situation. If the new
situation is the loss of all that is valuable, then the tradition is
finished. But if the situation is the "emergence of the human," then
the tradition is of great importance, because it provides the norms
and motivations for embracing the new situation relevantly and
responsibly. If the new situation is the emergence of the human,[19]
then we have recourse to the traditions to characterize the human.

The tradition shows us clearly what it means to be fully human.
The Biblical teaching on creation is an affirmation about what it
means to be human. It means to be free and responsible; to be
engaged in the management of history and "nature"; to be in control of subhuman creation (animals and machines); to be sensitive and open to the needs of the "brother," of all fellow men; to
be dependent upon and subject to the "hovering mystery" which
holds life together. The Israelite traditions of law and prophecy
instruct us that the human society is the one that is just and humane. It protects those who cannot claim what is due them. The
goals of the fully human society are for every person and not just
for those fortunate enough to guarantee their own well-being.

Of course, the tradition bears witness to Jesus of Nazareth as
the clue to what the human is really about, and the cross looms
large as the symbol of full humanity. The cross about which the

prophet must speak is the expression of the person so human that he invested himself fully in the humanity of others even to his own death.[20] This is not a sad song about martyrdom nor a death-wish but the affirmation that my own humanity is at the disposal of the humanity of my fellows. That dimension of the tradition has bearing now upon the meaning of "law and order," economic affluence, work and worth, public and private responsibility, life and death, the quest for peace, the knowledge explosion, and the whole cluster of crises around the fact of urbanization. It is the prophet who is charged with exploring the connections between these. The tradition serves to celebrate the possibility of humanness against all the demonic forces which would deprive us of our humanness.

It is ironic and significant that those who do not truly discern the current situation of crisis very often are also those who do not grasp the point of the tradition. If the present crisis appears to be an end of all things valuable, often coupled with it is the mistaken notion that the tradition is concerned with points of doctrine. The prophet must work on both fronts: to show that the present is a crisis about our humanness and to make clear that the tradition is really concerned with justice and wholeness,[21] with the emergence of the human and the conquest of the demonic.[22]

The prophet is charged with helping people to make intelligent, informed decisions and to show that the decisions which must be made in the present are matters of life and death. On many fronts today "believers" are being called to choose life or death (cf. Deut. 30:15-20) concerning "law and order" and responsible freedom, concerning economic theory and social pluralization and secularization, nationalism and integration, education and disarmament. The choices made by the institutional church are no doubt for life or death, for relevance or irrelevance. The decisions made by the church on these questions will determine if she is to be an effective agent of God in time to come or a ghost town for those who have withdrawn from history. A church that chooses to disregard the present situation and the relevance of the tradition is surely choosing death. As individuals, to choose to hold on to the old world which is surely gone is a decision for anger, anxiety, withdrawal, which probably is death. Conversely, to choose responsible involvement for the emergence of the human is to choose abundant life known in Jesus of Nazareth (John 10:10). Not to choose is also to choose, and probably is to choose death. The prophet does not make the choice for his people, nor does he coerce them in anger to make a certain choice. But his burden is to make the choices clear, the consequences as clear as possible, and the inevitability of choice plain (Ezek. 33:1-6). Unfortunately, the choice for life is often against our more parochial notions of life and happiness and freedom and security and success. But the choice must be faced!

The Mood of Prophetic Ministry

It is often thought that the prophet must attack the people to whom he speaks. This is based on the assumption that the covenant has been deliberately broken. Sometimes this may be the case; often it is not. The mood and tone of prophetic ministry are greatly dependent upon the intention of the believing community.

1. PROPHECY AND BROKEN COVENANT

There are times when the believing community has deliberately broken covenant. This is clear in the Biblical prophets, and it seems clear in our time. There are situations in which the believing community has known the right course of action and has refused. I suspect this is true in many communities in racial conflict. There can be little doubt that persons understand the general imperatives of the Gospel but elect to act against the claims of the Gospel because of the cost and risk involved. Or perhaps in wartime, the believing community has some notion of the claims of the Gospel but deliberately acts against the demands of covenant because of other loyalties of class or nation. The same may be true in personal relations. From time to time each of us is in a situation of anger, insecurity, embarrassment, where we know the demands of our covenant faith but cannot bring ourselves to pay what it costs to remain within covenant.

In such times as this, the prophetic dimension of faith must stress the consequences of covenant violation in terms of all our choices being life and death.[23] The community which embraces segregated patterns in racial conflict must know about the consequences of more conflict and perhaps violence, of guilt and social unrest. The national church which opts for national loyalties in conflict with the claims of covenant must know of the consequences of broken covenant in terms of injustice, which lead surely to fresh conflicts, intensified hatred, and the guarantee that peace becomes ever more remote. When in our personal lives we deliberately choose from the many varieties of death, we need to face from time to time the misery, isolation, guilt, and inner turmoil we choose for ourselves, to say nothing of the anguish of broken communication with our fellows.

But even in such situations, the consequences of broken covenant can be explored in moods other than anger. The prophetic task is not to alienate and tell people off but to enable them to see that they have violated their own professed self-understanding. The judgment which comes from God in the course of historical events is not hastened or delayed by "prophetic anger." The voice of prophecy is not the voice of destruction.[24] It has profound respect and love for the one addressed. The prophet believes in the ability of the one addressed to choose, and leaves him the freedom of making his own choices. He does not engage in a fear campaign to bring about a choice. He only asserts as clearly as he can that the covenant is a valid way of viewing history and that this view of history carries with it implications for our honoring or breaking covenant. But the real goal of the prophet is not to have people understand the death they have chosen. It is rather to enable them to change, to make a new choice and so re-enter covenant.[25] This means, in terms of the factors we have outlined, a clear discernment of the present, a fresh understanding of the relevance of the tradition, and a decision to let the tradition touch the situation in a life-giving way.

2. PROPHECY AND BEWILDERED COVENANT

But more often than not, we break covenant not because we willfully rebel but because we are always called to live in situations where the implications of covenant are not clear. We break covenant not because we want to or need to but because the new crisis always outruns the interpretation of covenant which we have at hand. Out of an agrarian faith, we break covenant in an urban situation not because we don't care any more but because the implications of covenant for the new situation are not at all clear to us. People who care about the faith are not so much wanting to be free of the gifts and claims of covenant as they are completely bewildered by what the covenant means for the present. It really is not clear what the demands for justice mean for our complex military establishment. It is not clear how to act on birth control when the tradition stresses the human. Many persons are ill-equipped with the faith-from-the-farm for the decisions of urban life where they now are. But they do not want to remain ill-equipped. They want to know. They want to make decisions for life. In our prophetic ministry we are called to the hard work of helping them engage their faith with their situation in effective ways.

(1) God's Deeds Are Still Happening

One of the primary dimensions of the covenant (see chapter I) is the affirmation that God has acted in gracious, liberating ways for his people and we can respond in gratitude. Of course, we all believe that about our past, but it is not so clear or easy in our new situation to affirm God's gracious liberating deeds in the present moment. It is not easy to see his actions; and if we do not see his actions, then we come up short on responses out of gratitude.

The prophet is one who points to God's new saving actions. Perhaps we have looked in the wrong places. We have wanted them to be in personal actions, in pleasant confrontations. But deeds of God in Scripture which evoke gratitude are something else. They are displays of power and civil disobedience (Exodus), wrenching and tearing away (return from exile), and suffering and death (the cross of Jesus). Our tradition calls us to look in the un-pleasant, perhaps threatening public issues for the deeds of God. And the prophet must discern these. They may be wrenching experiences like the Delta Ministry of the National Council of Churches; the freeing action of liberalizing abortion laws; the

Castro government, which has brought new opportunities to some and taken great property from others; new taxes for education and housing; the formation of the United Nations, which invites bold thinking about supra-nationalism. Of course, they also happen in more domestic and local actions; e.g., healed relations between persons and between groups, as well as community policies and government programs. But the prophet must risk pointing, for we shall not know gratitude unless we become aware of the reasons for gratitude. That which makes us grateful to God may on short term be against our vested interests. But the prophet calls us to choose, and there we may find life or death.

(2) God's Demands Are Still Pressing

The other major fact of the covenant is its stipulations (see chapter I). God declares that this we must do if we would live in covenant with him. Now, the believing community is quite aware of the demands of God, but these have gotten confused with romantic morality and pietistic individualism. God's demands have been perverted so that they do not go beyond being good and staying pure. But the demands of God which come out of our tradition do not stress goodness so much as involvement. They do not speak of purity but of responsibility. They do not speak of churchly obligations but of investment in the secular community. They do not speak of personal morality but of the public issues of justice and peace.

Obviously we have nothing in our tradition of faith which tells us God's demands on the vexing social questions mentioned above. But the prophet must clarify that even here the Lord of the covenant makes demands upon his covenant people. The covenant people cannot be indifferent to any of these issues, for that is to choose death. Admittedly, the prophet does not have competence to prescribe in all of these areas. But neither did the prophets of Israel. They seldom advised the kings specifically on what to do in terms of international politics. They simply insisted that God cares about justice and peace and left the responsible parties to implement the tradition in the crisis. So today the prophetic voice of the believing community must address every social question simply because we mean to live in covenant. We must declare the norms of justice and peace and inquire about their implementation. We must be clear that even here God wills something and we must face the life/death question.

The prophet is thus not only proclaimer but also enabler and teacher. Much of the believing community does not know that God's deeds may be discerned even in our urbanized present. Many do not know that God's demands are still operative even in the complexities of today. But these persons are neither hostile nor resistant. They are open and desperate. They are relieved when they learn that the faith of the fathers is still valid. They do not need to be "clobbered" but to be instructed and led, enabled to engage the faith and the situation for themselves. These dimensions of the problem suggest to covenant people the mood in which the prophetic ministry must be practiced, not only in their hostile brokenness but also in their eager bewilderment.

The Prophetic Vocation of the Church

We have talked about the prophetic office in terms of the leader of the community, the ordained official. We have done so because the "prophetic office" in Scripture has played a large role in our discussion.

1. ALL OF GOD'S PEOPLE AS PROPHETS

But the foregoing discussion has assumed that the community of faith is not composed of a prophetic leader and non-prophetic members. Rather, in the faithful believing community every member is a prophet (see Num. 11:29).[26] As the "prophetic official" is set apart by the rite (or sacrament) of ordination, so every believer is set apart as prophet in the sacrament of baptism. He shares with the "prophetic official" the opportunity and responsibility of being engaged prophetically in his history. No doubt it is true that the "prophetic official" has skills and training peculiarly his own. But so does every other "baptized prophet." The exercise of this prophetic function means the same thing for each member as for the "prophetic official." Each Christian must be engaged in the true discernment of our situation, in reflection upon the validity of the tradition in this situation, and in a decision to engage the tradition with the crisis for the sake of life. In the complexities of today, the gifts of every person are essential to this function and none can function without the efforts of all.

2. FAITH IN A POLITICAL IDIOM

When we speak of prophecy as we have been, we obviously do not mean random oracles. Rather, we are talking about a new way of life, a way of regarding the brother, a new discernment of ourselves, and a new investment in the history we share with our brother. Earlier in the discussion I have suggested that Israel rejected the religious idiom of her neighbors and elected to speak in a political idiom, the idiom of covenant treaty. Prophetic faith expressed in a political idiom, the idiom of most of Scripture, has important implications for the life of the church. They are implications which are foreign and strange to much of the life of the church. Though many more could be listed, here are some representative implications of the political idiom of prophetic faith:

(1) The joyous life is one of decisions. The prophetic function is to call men to decisions. Very often the worship and theology of the church have treated people as though they should not have to make decisions, were not capable of making them, and the church should protect them from decisions. With such an attitude, "religion" as expressed in Sunday morning activities is a form of withdrawal from the realm where decisions must be made. The political idiom asserts that decisions about historical questions are the very "stuff" of healthy, happy existence. Interestingly, much psychotherapy affirms the same view.[27]

(2) We have been made free to choose and entrusted with a world about which we may choose (Gen. 1:28-30). God has not put us in a world where we are his puppets. All this talk about choosing life or death means that we really have the option to choose it, not only for ourselves but for our whole world. On all kinds of social questions we can have it either way. And we are free to make choices and live with their consequences. God has not abandoned the world, but he has entrusted it to us. Nothing

human is automatic, but we are free to choose and to implement our choices.

(3) The moral life is the involved life.[28] The prophet in Israel or today never invites people to withdraw from history because it is too risky, dirty, or ambiguous. We have abroad in the church a faulty notion of morality which identifies goodness with uninvolvement. Not so the prophet or the prophetic community. The moral person is one who will risk involvements in those spots in history where he may be wrong or may be hurt. This is likely the key point of the political as over against the religious idiom.

(4) Because this is God's world, this is a good world meant to be enjoyed (see Gen. 1:31). We have been tempted by much perverted hymnody to think that "heaven is our home," and that this world is a bad, tempting place in which to live, so that one must be careful if not withdrawn. This has come to expression in all kinds of ghetto-like practices, notably, monasticism, our attitude toward art and science, and, in general, the Puritan ethic. Against this the prophetic faith of Scripture affirms that this world in all its parts is for our use and enjoyment. This does not mean that there are no dangers or temptations. But we are called to find joy and wholeness in this very world where the demonic always calls us away from our humanness.

(5) Because God is on the move,[29] change is not to be feared. It is the way of life. We must be open to it and not afraid of it. The religious idiom tends to view God as guarantor of the status quo, so that any change is an affront to God. This view gets expressed in our worship practices, the pews in which we sit, our preference for organ, no guitar, and the formalism which characterizes much of our "religious" life. Against this the political idiom knows that to stay alive is to change and grow and move. Just now we are caught with theologies and structures which work against change. To be sure, this does not mean that every change is an action of God, but at least we must seek to discern his purposes in changes before rejecting them. The problem has been illuminated by Emmanuel Mesthene:

> Teachers who have been brought up to cherish the stable must take the children of parents who have been brought up to cherish the

> stable, and try to teach them that the stable, the unchanging, is
> unreal, constraining, a false goal, and that they will survive in an
> age of change to the degree that they become familiar with change,
> feel comfortable with it, understand it, master and control it.[30]

Though his comment is addressed to another problem, it is quite in
keeping with the life style affirmed by Israel's prophets.

(6) We have been entrusted with this world. We are called to
care for it and are held accountable for it (Gen. 1:28-31). Our
theology of passivity and uninvolvement has deceived us into
thinking the world was given to us humans and we need only to
receive it and be grateful. But prophetic faith suggests that the world
is not only a gift. It is a task given us. And if we are to have a
human world, we must make it so.[31] Prayer has often been a sub-
stitute for responsible caring. Now it comes clear that if we are to
have peace, brotherhood, equality, justice, we must not simply
pray for them but must engage for them. We have confused God's
gifts and our responsibilities. This does not in any way minimize
the graciousness of Yahweh or detract from his Lordship, for he
makes it possible, he guarantees the limits and provides the opportunities and blesses and hallows our efforts. But he does not do
our work for us. This emphasis upon our responsibility for the
world has been clarified again by Mesthene:

> . . . [men] thus left their work undone. The churches, if only by
> default at first, sought to fill the void and do men's work for
> them—their knowing, their building, their ruling, and their moral
> judging. . . . The churches were doing Man's work.
>   Man's renewed confidence in himself means that he takes up
> his own burden again.[32]

It is extremely important to recognize that man doing his own
work is an act of faith and not of rebellion. God, according to the
prophets, wills us to care and be involved and not to leave it to
him. The tendency to let God do our work is not faith but abdi-
cation.

(7) Power is a good gift, to be used creatively and constructively.[33] This is inherent in the political idiom. Certainly the prophets were concerned about power, not to condemn it per se, but
to condemn its use in ways which broke covenant. The church per-

sistently suffers from a kind of "spiritualism" which believes that any form of power is bad, and therefore the church refuses to exercise power or to address the use of power in any significant way. The real question of power concerns its use for humane or demonic ends, and here the prophet must speak.

(8) Conflict is healthy when it faces authentic issues.[34] The prophets, following the pattern of Moses, engaged in power struggles to bring about social change. This, too, follows from the political idiom of Biblical faith. Again the church is quite afraid of conflict; we are polite and cautious and often dishonest. Or we tend to be so concerned with personal feelings and involvements that we do not face issues. This in turn supports our infatuation with the status quo and prevents a serious engagement of history which is the scene of life/death conflict.

We have moved some distance from our beginning point, which was the covenant form of Biblical faith. And yet the structure of Biblical faith in the pattern of a political treaty is not at all removed from the concerns of the role of the contemporary church. Prophecy in Israel always confronts us with a basic question: Is history really the moment when we must face up to God? And the answer we give and live is our choosing of life or death.

The urgency of prophetic ministry is affirmed in Ezekiel 18:31-32:

> "Why will you die, O house of Israel? For I have no pleasure in the death of any one, says the Lord GOD; so turn, and live."

This statement contains what is essential: It hints of the current situation which may lead to death. It affirms that Yahweh, God of the tradition, wills life. It urges a decision. Our prophetic ministry can do no more than put this urgent question in compelling ways.

Notes and Acknowledgments

I. THE COVENANT CONTEXT OF THE PROPHETS OF ISRAEL

1. A summary of scholarship on this topic is offered in R. E. Clements, *Prophecy and Covenant*, Studies in Biblical Theology 43 (Naperville, Ill.: Alec R. Allenson, Inc., 1965).

2. This approach has lessened the emphasis upon the personality and psychological processes of the prophetic phenomenon and has placed the emphasis rightly upon the substance of the message and its proclamation. See my discussion, "Tradition Engaged with Crisis," *Theology and Life*, Summer 1966, pp. 118 ff.

3. The literature which establishes this position is almost exclusively in German. Fortunately Gerhard von Rad's *Old Testament Theology*, Vol. I (Edinburgh: Oliver and Boyd Ltd., 1962) is now available in English. See also his *The Problem of the Hexateuch and Other Essays* (Oliver and Boyd Ltd., 1966), pp. 1-78.

4. The credo has its earliest formulations in Deut. 26:5-9; Deut. 6:20-23; and Joshua 24:2-13. It is more fully expressed in Pss. 78, 105, 106, 136, and Neh. 9. Any specific dating of these is precarious. But one may note from the content that Pss. 105 and 136 are more positive and probably earlier; that Ps. 78 is concerned with the Davidic establishment, which may be a clue to its origin; and Ps. 106 bears a great burden of sin which suggests affinities with Neh. 9, which is clearly later. Note also this confessional form in Acts 7.

5. See Walter Harrelson, "Guidance in the Wilderness," *Interpretation*, January 1959, pp. 24 ff.

6. On creation as salvation see von Rad, "The Theological Problem of the Old Testament Doctrine of Creation," *The Problem of the Hexateuch*, pp. 131 ff., and B. D. Napier, "On Creation-Faith in the Old Testament," *Interpretation*, January 1962, pp. 21 ff.

7. The relation of the older traditions to the Davidic claims is a difficult question. A good case can be made that the Davidic claims in part negate the older traditions or at least compete with them. However, such evidence as Psalm 78 which is in sympathy with the Davidic claims asserts that David and his dynasty are not a rival but an extension of the older covenant traditions. See Ronald Clements, *Abraham and David* (London: SCM Press Ltd., 1967), pp. 79 ff., and the materials cited there.

8. Second Samuel 7 brings to focus the theology of the Davidic establishment and so stands in a pivotal position in the tradition. Cf. Clements, *Abraham and David*, pp. 53 ff.

9. Otto Bächli, *Israel und die Völker*, pp. 70 ff., discusses the "weapons" by which Israel maintained herself in a hostile culture. The tradition func-

145

tions as such a weapon in the prophetic tradition to preserve the covenant community from syncretism and perversion. Creative handling of the tradition makes it possible for the community to be engaged with culture but not engulfed by it. For a summary of Bächli see E. W. Nicholson, *Deuteronomy and Tradition* (Philadelphia: Fortress Press, 1967), pp. 88 ff.

10. A thorough analysis of the legal collections is offered by Robert H. Pfeiffer, *Introduction to the Old Testament* (New York: Harper & Brothers, 1941), pp. 210 ff., though it needs great revision in light of recent discussion. Recently available in English is Martin Noth's *The Laws in the Pentateuch and Other Studies* (Edinburgh: Oliver and Boyd Ltd., 1966), which provides a context for appreciating "law."

11. Noth, *op. cit.*, speaks about the law as a way of establishing Yahweh's *exclusive* claim over Israel.

12. Hans-Joachim Kraus, *Worship in Israel* (Richmond: John Knox Press, 1966).

13. The literature in this field is enormous and growing. See a summary statement by G. E. Mendenhall, "Covenant," *IBD*, Vol. I, pp. 714 ff. The basic work has been by Mendenhall, Baltzer, Beyerlin, and McCarthy. Form analysis makes it increasingly clear that this basic structure dominates great portions of Scripture, even when the form is represented only in fragmentary ways.

14. Harvey H. Guthrie, Jr., *Israel's Sacred Songs* (New York: The Seabury Press, 1966), pp. 157 ff., has presented a clear statement of the contrast between these two stances in worship and life.

II. THE PROPHETS AND THE TRADITIONS OF COVENANT

1. See the recent discussion of David Noel Freedman, "Divine Commitment and Human Obligation," *Interpretation*, October 1964, pp. 419 ff., in which he distinguishes covenants stressing the responsibility of Yahweh and those stressing the vow of Israel. See also Clements, *Abraham and David*, pp. 79 ff.

2. Some scholars hold that Hosea 11:8-9 is not a departure from the tradition but is another assertion of the judgment of God. See G. S. Glanzman, "Two Notes: Am. 3, 15 and Os. 11, 8-9," CBQ, XXIII (1961), pp. 230-233, and Delbert R. Hillers, *Treaty-Curses and the Old Testament Prophets* (Rome: Pontifical Biblical Institute, 1964), pp. 75 ff. However, a strong case can be made for the usual rendering, reflected in the RSV. See James M. Ward, *Hosea: A Theology Commentary* (New York: Harper & Row, 1966), pp. 192 ff., for a perceptive treatment.

3. Another mention of the Jacob tradition is found in 12:12 in a difficult context. Here the use of the tradition is not clear, though its location in the context of true and false cult may be suggestive.

4. On the Baal-Peor (Beth-Peor) tradition see Norman C. Habel, *Yahweh Versus Baal* (New York: Bookman Associates, Inc., 1964), pp. 24 ff.

5. The motifs are set forth by Harrelson, *op. cit.* Hosea clearly deepens both the guilt and the dependence motifs.

6. See the helpful discussion of von Rad, "The Crisis Due to the Conquest," *Old Testament Theology*, Vol. I, pp. 15-35.

7. The twofold use of Israel shows that the central concern of the nar-

rative is the solidarity and well-being of the community. "Evil" is a disruption of that solidarity and well-being, and for the sake of the community, the offender must be eliminated. Cf. Deut. 13:5; 17:7; 19:13, 18-19; 21:21; 22:21, 22, 23-24; 24:7 in reference to violation of the community. See the juxtaposition of these two words in Jer. 29:11; 38:4.

8. Failure to recognize what it means to be Israel is closely related to "knowledge of God," a prominent theme in Hosea. Wolff, " 'Wissen um Gott,' bei Hosea als Urform von Theologie," *Gesammelte Studien zum Alten Testament,* p. 195, writes: "To 'knowledge' belongs in germ a teaching of distinctiveness, which clarifies who is Yahweh and who is Baal, who has a claim to Israel and what the consequences of it are." Cf. Isa. 1:3b; Jer. 4:22.

The dimensions of covenant implied in "knowledge" which were anticipated by Wolff have now been substantiated by H. B. Huffmon, "The Treaty Background of Hebrew *Yāda'*," *BASOR* 181, February 1966, pp. 31 ff. For a similar expression of misunderstanding of the community, see 1 Cor. 11:29 and the admonition to "discern the body."

9. See von Rad, "The Crisis Due to the Formation of the State," *Old Testament Theology,* Vol. I, pp. 36-68.

10. See von Rad's pertinent comments, *ibid.,* p. 25, on the urgency of saying "No" to Canaanization. The problem then as now is that "Canaanization" is so attractive and natural. It happens so gradually that it is scarcely noticed until it is a *fait accompli.*

11. The prophetic use of legal traditions in Amos has been analyzed by Robert Bach, "Gottesrecht und Weltliches Recht in der Verkündigung des Propheten Amos," *Festschrift für Günther Dehn,* ed. by Wilhelm Schneemelcher, pp. 23 ff.; in Micah by Walter Beyerlin, *Die Kulttraditionen Israels in der Verkündigung des Propheten Micha;* and in a broader way in Ezekiel by H. Graf Reventlow, *Wächter über Israel.*

12. See the summary of legal forms in Claus Westermann, *Basic Forms of Prophetic Speech* (Philadelphia: The Westminster Press, 1967).

13. See von Rad, "The Veto on Images in the Old Testament," *Old Testament Theology,* Vol. I, pp. 212-219, in which he shows that the prohibition concerns a whole other view of history, over which Israel affirms Yahweh's total sovereign freedom. The commandment is concerned with how Israel regarded history.

14. See Dorothea Ward Harvey, "Rejoice Not, O Israel!," in *Israel's Prophetic Heritage,* ed. by Bernhard W. Anderson and Walter Harrelson (New York: Harper & Brothers, 1962), pp. 116 ff.

15. Though the text is not clear, the verb is the same one used in Exod. 20:13.

16. On Hosea's opposition to the priesthood of his time, see especially H. W. Wolff, "Hoseas geistige Heimat," *TLZ* 81, 1956, col. 83 ff., in which he relates Hosea to the conservative Levitical circle of tradition. This explains both his opposition and his reliance upon the traditions as the basis for opposition.

17. The proclamation of Hosea, as in the other prophets, employs much of the imagery and language of the court. See Herbert B. Huffmon, "The Covenant Lawsuit in the Prophets," *JBL,* December 1959, pp. 285 ff., and

Julien Harvey, "Le Rib-Pattern, Requisitoire prophetique sur la Rupture de L'Alliance," *Biblica* 1962, pp. 172 ff., for this line of reasoning.

18. See especially A. Alt, "Die Heimat des Deuteronomiums," *Kleine Schriften zur Geschichte des Volkes Israel II,* pp. 250 ff.

19. Bächli, *op. cit.,* has made this point most clearly. See especially pp. 56 ff. Deut. 7 refers to "many nations" whereas Hosea speaks of "strangers," but the main point is the same; cf. Deut. 25:5. Deut. 7 is positively concerned with Israel as a holy people. Hosea's polemic against foreign involvement is best understood in this context. The concept "holy people" in Deut. 14:1-21 is used in this way as a polemic against syncretism.

20. This translation is suggested in *BH,* ed. Kittel. See Aubrey R. Johnson, *The Vitality of the Individual in the Thought of Ancient Israel* (Cardiff: University of Wales Press, 1949), pp. 75 ff.

21. The indictment "They did not listen," is prominent in Jeremiah (see 7:24, 26, 27; 36:31; 37:2). On the basis of this indictment, the collapse of 587 B.C. is grounded. A. K. Fenz, *Auf Jahwes Stimme Hören,* has summarized the evidence and has shown how central this motif is for understanding covenant.

22. Brevard S. Childs, *Memory and Tradition in Israel* (London: SCM Press, 1962), pp. 45 ff., has made clear how important memory is to Israel. It is not simply recollection but is the appropriation of past tradition for the present. In this way Israel discerns what it means to be Israel in the new situation. Without this reference to the past, Israel has no context in which to live in the present.

23. The note sounded in Exodus 22:28b should be mentioned, but it plays no part in the later development of an attitude toward kingship. On the political message of Hosea, see Norman K. Gottwald, *All the Kingdoms of the Earth* (New York: Harper & Row, 1964), pp. 119 ff.

24. So Noth, *The Laws in the Pentateuch,* p. 18, Deut. 17: 14-20, writes: ". . . but it is clear that it occurs here primarily because what underlay the law-code was *not* state regulations concerned with the institution of monarchy, but rather another system on whose basis the then existing institution of kingship is in fact criticized." That other "system" is of course the older covenant ordering of community life which has been called "amphyctyony."

25. In "Amos iv 4-13 and Israel's Covenant Worship," *VT,* January 1965, pp. 1 ff., I have shown that the cult polemic of Amos 4:4-5 is an integral part of the indictment. The same is true in this passage.

26. The definitive treatment of this text is by Alt, *ibid.,* pp. 163 ff. Recently Edwin M. Good, "Hosea 5:8—6:6: An Alternative to Alt," *JBL,* September 1966, pp. 273 ff., has demonstrated the legal, liturgic context of the passage. He notes that the passage must also be set in relation to the curse of Deut. 27:17. The indictment and curse mean that the princes of Judah "are here being declared 'beyond the pale' of the covenant by their transgression of its law" (p. 277).

27. The imagery of harlotry as applied to the Yahweh-Israel relationship is obviously not the primary one in the old traditions. The dominant one is clearly the king-servant motif. This has been recently examined in some depth by Edward F. Campbell, Jr., "Sovereign God" (Inaugural Address),

McCormick Quarterly, March 1967, pp. 173 ff., and earlier by G. E. Wright, "How Did Early Israel Differ from Her Neighbors?" *BA*, February 1943, pp. 1 ff., and "The Terminology of Old Testament Religion and Its Significance," *JNES*, January-October, 1942, pp. 404 ff.

28. Noth, *The Laws in the Pentateuch*, p. 51, has shown how the covenant ideology revolves around the exclusiveness of the relationship: The laws "are provisions which seek to ensure the exclusive nature of the relationship between God and people, between Yahweh and the Israelite tribes, or (in other words) which guard against a defection in any form from the sole God, who is thought of as a partner to the covenant. The history of religions by and large knows nothing of this concept of 'defection,' because it is solely a consequence of a strict requirement of restriction to a single God." The prophet works with the defection theme, for which the imagery of harlotry is well-suited.

29. This profound understanding of the helplessness of the sinner in the face of his infidelity, so clearly stated by Hosea, also appears in 2 Esdras 7:48 and Romans 7:24. The imagery of Hosea lends itself to a vivid statement.

III. THE PROPHETS AND THE COVENANT FORMS

1. See James Muilenburg, "The 'Office' of the Prophet in Ancient Israel," *The Bible in Modern Scholarship*, ed. by J. Philip Hyatt (Nashville: Abingdon Press, 1965), pp. 94 ff.

2. Indicative of this is the rarity with which Claus Westermann, *Basic Forms of Prophetic Speech* (Philadelphia: The Westminster Press, 1967), cites texts from Hosea. On p. 181 he speaks of a "relaxation" of form in Hosea. This likely suggests the freedom with which the prophet handles traditional materials. But it certainly cannot be viewed as an absence of form.

3. For very brief summaries on prophetic forms see James Muilenburg, "Old Testament Prophecy," p. 478, and E. T. Ryder, "Form Criticism of the Old Testament," pp. 91 ff., *Peake's Commentary on the Bible* (London: Thomas Nelson and Sons Ltd., 1962). Claus Westermann, *Basic Forms of Prophetic Speech*, now has provided the best discussion of forms we have in English. Unfortunately Westermann only considers certain of the forms. Nevertheless he provides a thorough introduction to the study of forms.

4. Westermann, *op. cit.*, p. 130, has delineated this form. On pages 170-181 he shows how general statements are characteristically developed by more specific statements so that any misunderstanding is precluded. Thus the form develops with a precision not unexpected in a legal brief.

5. Jared J. Jackson, "Yahweh v. Cohen et al.," *Pittsburgh Perspective*, 1966, pp. 28 ff., has offered a detailed, convincing analysis of Hosea 4 as a complete lawsuit form.

6. Of the terms employed in this indictment, most are well attested in the old legal traditions as a concern of covenant relationship. Thus the spilling of blood is dealt with (Deut. 19:6, 12; 21:8-9). There is warning against defilement (Lev. 18:23), wickedness (Lev. 18:17; 19:29; 20:14), and pervasive interest in the matter of harlotry (Exod. 34:15-16; Lev. 17:7; 19:29; 20:5; 21:7, 9, 14; Deut. 22:21; 23:18). Obviously the prohibition on

murder is rooted in the decalogue (Exod. 20:13). The term rendered "banded together" is nowhere known in the old traditions, and so stands outside the connection to the old laws. The term rendered "evildoers" is difficult. It is not mentioned in the old traditions and yet is well-known in the cultic literature of the Psalms. Mowinckel, *Psalmenstudien I,* and J. Pedersen, *Israel: Its Life and Culture, I-II* (London: Oxford University Press, 1926), pp. 430 ff., connect it with practices of witchcraft, while Harris Birkeland, *The Evildoers in the Book of Psalms* (Oslo: I Kommisjon hos Jacob Dybwad, 1955), relates it to the political, historical enemies of Israel. Johnson, "The Psalms," *OTMS,* pp. 197 ff., takes a more cautious view which gives the term a general meaning, putting it back into the context of covenant. Thus, while several of the terms taken separately are problematic, the total cluster makes it clear that we are given a description of those who flagrantly violate covenant. The point to be made here is that the bill of particulars is an explication of the general indictment of vs. 7.

7. Vs. 12b which alludes to Judah scarcely fits the context. Thus we may read "Jacob" (cf. 12:2a), or perhaps the line is an intrusion. See Ward, *Hosea: A Theological Commentary,* pp. 209 f., for another solution.

8. Most commentators read "Israel." It is not clear that vs. 2 belongs with 11:12—12:1, but it may look backward as well as forward.

9. The use of the particle has been examined in great detail by James Muilenburg, "The Linguistic and Rhetorical Usages of the Particle *ki* in the Old Testament," *HUCA* 1961, pp. 135 ff.

10. H. W. Wolff, "Die Begründungen der prophetischen Heilsund Unheilssprüche," *ZAW* 1934, pp. 1-22 (*Gesammelte Studien,* pp. 9 ff.), has shown that the "basis" for the sentence may either precede or follow the sentence itself.

11. In Hosea 4:4-19, the particle "surely" occurs at four strategic places to mark emphases in the unit, vss. 6, 10, 14, and 16. Unfortunately they are not adequately reflected in our English translations.

12. The text is corrupt, but this is a cogent reconstruction accepted by many commentators.

13. That this indictment belongs properly in a context of covenant is suggested by recent study of the word "good" in treaty documents. See W. L. Moran, *CBQ,* January 1963, p. 79, n. 15, and *JNES,* July 1963, pp. 173 ff.; A. Malamat, *BA,* May 1965, pp. 63 f.; and D. R. Hillers, "A Note on Some Treaty Terminology in the Old Testament," *BASOR,* 176, December 1964, pp. 46 f.

14. James Muilenburg, "The Form and Structure of the Covenantal Formulations," *VT,* October 1959, pp. 347 ff., has noted the structural importance of this particle as it forms a link between proclamation and exhortation. It may not be unimportant that the same word used in the covenant formula is employed in the covenant indictment. The particle "now" in Hosea 5:3 is strengthened further by its pairing with "surely." On this combination of particles see Muilenburg, "Usages of the Particle," p. 138.

15. Westermann, *op. cit.,* pp. 66 ff.

16. This continuity between sentence and curse has been carefully considered and elaborated by Delbert R. Hillers, *Treaty-Curses and the Old*

Testament Prophets, where the problem is considered in relation to the extra-Biblical materials. The relevant literature is cited there. Of special interest is the work of F. Charles Fensham, "Common Trends in Curses of the Near Eastern Treaties and *Kudurru*-Inscriptions Compared with Maledictions of Amos and Isaiah," *ZAW,* 75 (1963), pp. 155-175, and "Malediction and Benediction in Ancient Near Eastern Vassal-Treaties and the Old Testament," *ZAW,* 74 (1962), pp. 1-9.

17. This point is also acknowledged by Westermann, *op. cit.,* pp. 194 ff. On p. 153 he notes the profane language of the sentence, and on p. 197 he correctly says that the curse "has lost its impersonal magical character." From this he draws the conclusion on p. 153 that "not a trace of cultic language can be found." In the next chapter I will attempt to redefine Israel's cult in a way that permits the indictment-sentence form to be understood as having a cultic context. Westermann consistently rejects such a suggestion, but operates with an understanding of cult that is open to question.

18. Hillers, *op. cit.,* pp. 30 ff., presents a convincing case for the unity and antiquity of these chapters against the traditional dissections of literary critics. Leviticus 26 has been studied especially by Reventlow, *Das Heiligkeitsgesetz,* pp. 142 ff., and utilized in his subsequent studies of Amos, Jeremiah, and Ezekiel. Deuteronomy 28:3-6, 16-19 has been carefully analyzed by Erik Morstad, *Wenn du der Stimme des Herrn, deines Gottes, gehorchen wirst.* The work by Hillers suggests that much more remains to be done on each of them.

19. Westermann, *op. cit.,* pp. 149 ff.

20. Westermann, *op. cit.,* p. 152, claims that the "I-speech" is derived from the announcement of salvation. The conclusions he draws from this depend upon a certain notion of cult which Westermann does not clarify.

21. Westermann, *op. cit.,* p. 149, suggests that "therefore behold" can replace the messenger formula and function in the same way. Perhaps the simple "therefore" has a similar role. It is certainly emphatic and gives authority to the announcement that follows.

22. See Hillers, *op. cit.,* pp. 54 ff. He mentions in this connection 5:12, which also refers to God under the simile "moth."

23. It is now clear that the mention of exile need not be post-587 B.C., for the threat of exile was included in the very ancient treaty curses and so can be early in the Israelite tradition. See Dennis J. McCarthy, *Treaty and Covenant* (Rome: Pontifical Biblical Institute, 1963), pp. 122 ff., and Hillers, *op. cit.,* pp. 33 ff. One element in the curse of exile is a "return to Egypt." For a close parallel to Hosea 9:3, 6 and 11:5, see Deut. 28:68.

24. McCarthy, *Der Gottesbund im Alten Testament,* p. 61, gives a brief summary of the relevant literature.

25. See the important discussion by Erhard Gerstenberger, "The Woe-Oracles of the Prophets," *JBL,* September 1962, pp. 249 ff., in which he finds behind the prophetic use of the term the context of the clan ethos which has most in common with what is called the wisdom traditions. He then suggests the process by which this received new authority and solemnity in prophetic use. For a more conventional and simpler explanation, see Westermann, *op. cit.,* pp. 190 ff.

26. The precise relationship between guilt and punishment is a very difficult matter. Klaus Koch, "Gibt es ein Vergeltungsdogma Alten Testament," *ZTK* 1955, pp. 1 ff., argues that there is a "sphere of destiny" in which the very deed itself set in motion the punishment and guaranteed it. Indeed, the faithfulness of Yahweh is expressed in the fact that the two do correspond (Ps. 62:12), (p. 21). Against this H. Graf Reventlow, "Sein Blut komme über sein Haupt," *VT* 1960, p. 311, argues that in the faith of Israel, the Lordship of Yahweh stands between guilt and punishment so that the correspondence is not necessarily one-to-one.

27. Claus Westermann, "The Way of the Promise through the Old Testament," in *The Old Testament and Christian Faith*, ed. by Bernhard W. Anderson (New York: Harper & Row, 1963), pp. 200-224.

28. Westermann, "The Way of the Promise," pp. 206-208, defines the announcement of salvation as an assertion in a future (imperfect) verb of an action which is only promised but not yet realized. Thus it has a hint of uncertainty that a past action does not have. The pure form as Westermann characterizes it leaves no room for a phrase introduced by "surely." The adverb functions as a kind of statement of basis: "Surely my anger has turned from me." The departure from the strict form shows that the promise-speech is a response to a situation of broken covenant which calls for an indictment-sentence. By a very curious turn the prophet employs this "inappropriate" form. This alteration of form communicates an important message.

29. Westermann, "The Way of the Promise," pp. 208-211, characterizes the "portrayal" as a description of the new situation of salvation. It is not speech about an act but a new condition resulting from a salvation act. Note that in this example, the form varies in terms of singular and plural without any intended change in meaning.

30. As we have indicated, the messenger formula may be replaced by other formal elements as Westermann, *Basic Forms*, p. 149, observes. He speaks of this change in terms of the lawsuit, but in this passage it also occurs with a promise-oracle.

31. Westermann, "The Way of the Promise," pp. 202-205, describes this as an announcement of salvation in perfect verbs so that the action is already completed. The form therefore suggests a high degree of certitude. It is the strongest of Westermann's three types and obviously functions in a decisive way for Hosea.

32. This characterization of the form is not in Westermann's analysis. It is most like his "portrayal," and yet that is scarcely an adequate term. It is closer to promise than to blessing, i.e., dynamic rather than stative, yet it lacks the "I-speech." I suggest it is a separate kind of form which functions to mark the complete reversal of the covenant relationship. It not only speaks of the covenant but sets the promise-speech in the context of covenant to a much greater extent than Westermann is inclined to think. The fuller form of this element is apparent in Jeremiah and Ezekiel, "I shall be your God and you will be my people." But already in Hosea, we begin to have indications that restoration is the most important of the anticipations held out to Israel. It occurs in a climactic position in Isa. 51:16, and in the salvation portrayal of Rev. 21: 1-4 it occupies an important place in vs. 3. This element maintains the portrayal in the context of covenant.

33. We have seen few formal elements which mark this form. Here is a good example of future orientation both at the beginning and the end of the unit. Probably it functions much like "in that day" in 2:16-23. There is no hint of eschatology here. Rather this formal element serves to contrast in radical terms the previous condition of brokenness and the anticipated restoration. It is this contrast rather than emphasis on time which is expressed in the form.

34. On healing see the very old statement of Exod. 15:26b, which belongs in a tradition very much like the antecedents of Hosea. William L. Moran, "The Ancient Near Eastern Background of the Love of God in Deuteronomy," *CBQ*, January 1963, pp. 77-87, has shown that "love" refers to a treaty concept of mutual fidelity. The word in our text suggests a guarantee of covenant renewal.

35. This declaration draws upon Holy War tradition which stresses the power of Yahweh as distinct from human armaments. If this is so, it further supports the context of Hosea in the old Northern traditions; cf. Zech. 4:6 and the discussion of von Rad, *Der Heilige Krieg im Alten Israel*, pp. 66 ff. He summarizes the Holy War motif: "Not arms preparation, but Yahweh." H. W. Wolff has claimed that Hosea stands in Levitical circles, "Hoseas geistige Heimat," *TLZ* 1956, pp. 83-94. If that is true and if von Rad, *Studies in Deuteronomy* (Chicago: Henry Regnery Co., 1953), pp. 66 ff., is correct in linking the Levites and Holy War, the presence of this motif and form in Hosea is not surprising.

36. This point has been well made by David Noel Freedman, "Divine Commitment and Human Obligation," *Interpretation*, October 1964, pp. 430-431. See also Ronald Clements, *Abraham and David*, pp. 79 ff.

37. Westermann, *Basic Forms*, pp. 184 ff., argues that this is not a primary prophetic form. In light of the recent study of Tom Raitt (unpublished dissertation at Vanderbilt), that may now be questioned. In any case it is clear that the call to repentance has an important part to play in the prophetic message and, as Westermann suggests, has firm roots in the covenant tradition.

38. *Amos' Geistige Heimat,* pp. 30 ff.

39. J. Wijngaards, "Death and Resurrection in Covenantal Context (Hos. vi 2)," *VT*, April 1967, pp. 237 f., has described the close relation between covenant renewal and the restoration of fertility among other blessings.

40. This understanding of the text has recently been clarified by J. Wijngaards, *op. cit.,* pp. 226 ff. He argues that the death of vs. 2 is the removal of the vassal from his position of favor, and to "revive" and "raise up" is restoration in a favorable covenant relation. Edwin M. Good, *op. cit.,* pp. 273 ff., has shown that the text belongs in a liturgical context and is concerned with covenant renewal.

41. *Amos' Geistige Heimat,* pp. 30 ff.

42. *Wesen und Herkunft des "Apodiktischen Rechts,"* pp. 109 ff., and *passim.* See also W. Richter, *Recht und Ethos,* pp. 54 ff.

43. See the caution of J. L. Crenshaw, "The Influence of the Wise upon Amos," *ZAW* 1967, pp. 48 ff., and his reference to the criticism of Reventlow, *ZTK* 1963, pp. 267 ff. Wolff, "Hoseas Geistige Heimat," *TLZ* 1956, col. 83-94, has located Hosea in a quite different tradition. See also Muilenburg,

"The 'Office' of the Prophet in Ancient Israel," *The Bible in Modern Scholar-ship*, ed. by J. P. Hyatt, pp. 93 ff.

44. Westermann, *Basic Forms*, pp. 184 ff., suggests this connection though he does not pursue the question. Erhard Gerstenberger seems to support this in "Jeremiah's Complaints," *JBL*, December 1963, p. 397, n. 17.

45. In his comment on Hosea 6, Edwin Good, *op. cit.*, pp. 285-286, draws a connection between that call to repentance and the dialogue of Joshua 24:14 ff., which obviously is concerned with covenant making. The discussion of Wijngaards, *op. cit.*, also makes a connection between an original allegiance which is exclusive and later renewal which is a return to that allegiance.

46. See Good, *op. cit.*, pp. 285 f.

47. The use of the word "office" is, of course, problematic. The question will be considered in detail in the next chapter. Here I mean simply that the prophet had an identifiable role and function which informed his self-understanding. That role and function was concerned with broken and restored covenant. For a summary of recent discussion, see D. McCarthy, *Der Gottesbund im Alten Testament*, pp. 58 ff.

48. H. Graf Reventlow, *Wächter über Israel*, pp. 116 ff.

49. Westermann, *Basic Forms*, p. 19.

50. See Raitt, unpublished dissertation, Vanderbilt.

IV. THE PROPHETS AND THE COVENANT INSTITUTION

1. See von Rad, *Old Testament Theology*, Vol. II. He structures his theology around the poles of "The Theology of Israel's Historical Traditions" (Vol. I) and "The Theology of Israel's Prophetic Traditions" (Vol. II). R. E. Clements, *Prophecy and Covenant*, has offered a more popular presentation of the theme.

2. There is general agreement among scholars on the first two lines of evidence which have been considered. However, it is by no means so clear that it necessarily follows that the place of the traditions and the forms must be the cult. See especially the caution of Georg Fohrer, "Remarks on Modern Interpretation of the Prophets," *JBL*, December 1961, p. 312, where he distinguishes between the responsible use of form criticism and its use for "cultic fantasies." Erhard Gerstenberger, "The Woe-Oracles of the Prophets," *JBL*, September 1962, p. 262, n. 42, suggests that the prophets spoke very much out of the "popular ethos" of the time and that it was not necessary to assume a cultic background for the oracles of the prophets.

Part of the hesitation about placing the prophet in a cultic setting is the fear that the personality of the prophet will be minimized. This concern has been expressed by Fohrer and Muilenburg. In chapter V, I will seek to show that this is not a necessary consequence of the close relation of cult and prophet.

3. This has been clearly presented by John Bright ("Modern Study of Old Testament Literature") and George E. Mendenhall ("Biblical History in Transition") in their essays in *The Bible and the Ancient Near East*, edited by G. E. Wright (Garden City, N. Y.: Doubleday & Co., Inc., 1961), pp. 13 ff., 32 ff.

4. This set of assumptions, though seldom stated, is amply attested in

recent seminary curricula and the educational life of the church generally. It is worth noting that Liberal Jewish interpreters have their own version of this same evolutionary theory. Thus it is said that the prophets are "the creators of Judaism," again suggesting that the older religion of the Torah has been displaced.

5. Rudolf Bultmann regards the Old Testament as a history of failure. As a result, it has no distinctive role at all in his understanding of Christian faith and may even be a different religion. See his statement and a variety of responses in *The Old Testament and Christian Faith*, edited by B. W. Anderson.

6. John Greenleaf Whittier.

7. It is interesting to note that as Protestant scholars are now rediscovering the communal dimension of the prophets which had been lost or minimized for a century, at the same time Roman Catholic scholars are stressing the ethical, "over-againstness" of the prophet which had not been appreciated by the more traditional scholars of that church. Thus, for example, see Bruce Vawter, *The Conscience of Israel* (New York: Sheed and Ward, Inc., 1961).

8. The "man against the system" understanding of the prophet has provided the dominant image by which many ministers understand themselves and their work. Clearly this image deprives the minister of the support and resources which are otherwise available to him in the tradition and in institutional forms.

9. Mowinckel, *Religion und Kultus*, p. 13. On the peculiarly Israelite dimensions of cult, see H. J. Kraus, "Gottesdienst im alten und im neuen Bund," *EvTh* 1965, pp. 171-206, and Martin J. Buss, "The Meaning of 'Cult' and the Interpretation of the Old Testament," *JBR*, October 1964, pp. 317 ff.

10. This has been clear since the study of R. Dussaud, *Les Origines Cananéennes du Sacrifice Israélite*, 1921. More recent evidence gives additional decisive support to his thesis.

11. Harvey Guthrie, *Israel's Sacred Songs*, pp. 157 ff., has suggested some of the distinctive points in Israel's worship. This offers an important corrective to a more general characterization of cult, as for example in Mowinckel.

12. I have developed this theme in my dissertation, "A Form-Critical Study of the Cultic Material in Deuteronomy: An Analysis of the Nature of Cultic Encounter in the Mosaic Tradition" (Union Seminary, New York, 1961), pp. 170 ff. See the exposition of Kraus, "Gottesdienst im alten und im neuen Bund," *EvTh* 1965, pp. 171 ff., in which he considers the main characteristics of Israel's worship as it points toward the worship of the New Testament Church.

13. A most prominent and unfortunate failure to grasp this fact is the discussion of cult by Ludwig Koehler, *Old Testament Theology* (London: Lutterworth Press, 1957), pp. 181 ff., which he entitles "Man's Expedient for His Own Redemption: The Cult." He claims, p. 195, that "Until the time of Ezekiel the cult does not belong to the Old Testament revelation." Koehler does not reckon with the distinctiveness of the cult of Israel which results because it is placed in the context of and made a vehicle of the covenant.

14. Of this Buss, *op. cit.*, p. 322, can write: "In Israelite cult, the God-man relation is not natural, in the sense that it is given. There is a requirement for decision; laws are decreed; threats and promises support allegiance. In a personal way, God and man stand confronting each other." What is new in Israel's cult is that now worship is structured and expressed, dramatized and verbalized, in covenant terms.

15. H. H. Rowley, "Ritual and the Hebrew Prophets," *Myth, Ritual, and Kingship*, ed. by S. H. Hooke (Oxford: Oxford University Press, 1958), pp. 236 ff., has offered a characteristically balanced, cautious discussion. In my judgment, form analysis has advanced since his essay, so that his extreme caution is unwarranted.

16. See my suggestion concerning the polemic of Amos 4:4-5 in "Amos iv 4-13 and Israel's Covenant Worship," *VT*, January 1965, pp. 8 ff., and J. Philip Hyatt, *The Prophetic Criticism of Israelite Worship* (Goldenson Lecture, 1963).

17. The mediatorial function of Moses is abundantly clear. See George E. Mendenhall, *Law and Covenant in Israel and the Ancient Near East* (Pittsburgh: The Biblical Colloquium, 1955), pp. 47 ff., and von Rad, *Old Testament Theology*, Vol. I, pp. 294 ff. It is quite incidental that Mendenhall sees Moses in royal terms (cf. J. R. Porter, *Moses and Monarchy: A Study in the Biblical Tradition of Moses* [Oxford: Basil Blackwell, 1963]) and von Rad presents Moses in prophetic terms. Moses' function is to mediate and so negotiate a treaty and keep it in repair. When the covenant is broken, i.e., when death is due Israel, his function is to find a way whereby life can be given. To bring life where death is due he may (a) seek Yahweh's change of heart (intercession), see Exod. 32:11-14, or (b) seek Israel's change of heart (call to repentance), see Deut. 10:12-22. His function is to be concerned with the life/death struggle to maintain the covenant (see Deut. 30:15-20).

18. See especially Rolf Rendtorff, "Reflections on the Early History of Prophecy in Israel," *History and Hermeneutic*, Vol. IV of *Journal for Theology and the Church*, ed. by Funk and Ebeling (New York: Harper & Row, 1967), pp. 14 ff.

19. See Mendenhall, *op. cit.*, pp. 31 ff., for a list of the factors in covenant making. As the one responsible for the covenant, the mediator presumably has a role in each part of covenant making. Kraus, *Die prophetische Verkündigung des Rechts in Israel*, pp. 12 ff., and *passim*, presents the Mosaic role in a rigorously institutional way.

20. Among recent discussions on the relationship between Moses and the prophets, in addition to that of Kraus are: James Muilenburg, "The 'Office' of the Prophet in Ancient Israel," *The Bible in Modern Scholarship*, ed. by P. Hyatt, pp. 74 ff.; R. Rendtorff, "Erwägungen zur Frühgeschichte des Prophetentums in Israel," *ZTK* 1962, pp. 145 ff.; H. G. Reventlow, "Prophetenamt und Mittleramt," *ZTK* 1961, pp. 269 ff.; and Erhard Gerstenberger, "Jeremiah's Complaints: Observations on Jer. 15:10-21," *JBL*, December 1963, pp. 405 ff.

21. As concerns Hosea, see the analysis of H. W. Wolff, "Hoseas geistige Heimat," *ThLZ* 1956, pp. 83-94. A careful and balanced critique of Wolff's hypothesis is offered by Rendtorff, *op. cit.*, pp. 19 ff.

22. The term "office" has been used by Muilenburg, Reventlow, and Kraus, and by Martin Noth, "Office and Vocation in the Old Testament," in his *The Laws in the Pentateuch and Other Studies,* pp. 229 ff. The precise meaning of the term in such contexts is difficult and we must take care not to run beyond the evidence. It does seem possible at least to say that the community as having a certain authority and "officer" is recognized in the community as having a certain authority and that he is charged with a certain responsibility. We can speak of a free non-institutional prophecy if we say the prophet only condemns broken covenant. But if he also repairs and renews covenant, as seems clear, then he must in some way be involved in the public instrument of renewal, namely, the cult.

23. Reventlow, *Liturgie und prophetisches Ich bei Jeremia,* pp. 24 ff., has handled the call of Jeremiah in this way, without denying the authenticity of the personal experience.

24. This is how it was with Moses (Exod. 20:19; Deut. 5:27), and is the meaning of the prophetic formula, "The word of the LORD came . . ." Cf. Reventlow, "Prophetenamt und Mittleramt," pp. 272 f., and *passim.* This is why the indictment, "You did not listen," is so serious; e.g., Jer. 35:17. The rejection of the prophetic word is rejection of Yahweh's word. The prophet is an authoritative mediator. For a like situation see 1 Sam. 8:7.

25. See von Rad, *Old Testament Theology,* Vol. II, pp. 70 ff., for an exposition of the problem.

26. The oracle of Hosea which is usually included in the list of prophetic polemics against cult is in 6:4-6. As Wolff, *op. cit.,* pp. 84 ff., rightly concludes, the prophet is not attacking the cult but speaks out of very ancient cultic traditions against the contemporary perversion of the cult. The great words we have often taken to be the prophetic words are in fact the great words of the covenant cult. Wolff traces these back to the Levitical circles of Deuteronomy which in turn go back to the Mosaic tradition. That the passage concerns restoration of covenant has been persuasively argued by Edwin Good, "Hosea 5:8—6:6: An Alternative to Alt," *JBL,* September 1966, pp. 273 ff., and J. Wijngaards, "Death and Resurrection in Covenantal Context (Hos. vi 2)," *VT,* April 1967, pp. 226 ff.

27. Though the false prophets may have been linked to the cult, it is not this fact which makes them false prophets. Von Rad, "Die falschen Propheten," *ZAW* 1933, pp. 109 ff., suggests that because the cult prophet must affirm that Yahweh is among his people in the cult place, the people are safe from any harm and, therefore, the prophet in the cult must always speak "well-being." And to speak "well-being" when Yahweh is to bring judgment is what makes the prophet false. Presumably, von Rad would modify this in light of the subsequent discussion. See the recent summary by Eva Osswald, *Falsche Prophetie im Alten Testament.*

28. Thus, for example, Deut. 18:20-22. The criterion here is whether the prophet's word comes true or not. This can be interpreted so that authority is judged by "power to predict." However, it is also possible to view this measure in a much more sophisticated way. The true prophet is one who has discerned how Yahweh characteristically acts in history and so can proclaim his action which is yet to happen. The prophet who does not speak rightly about the future has not discerned Yahweh's ways of acting and so

is false. Set in the terms of our argument, he has not rightly understood the relation between the covenant and historical events.

29. This way of formulating the proposition is borrowed from Prof. James Muilenburg.

30. This perspective has been a primary contribution of von Rad; see his *The Problem of the Hexateuch*, pp. 26 ff., and Kraus, *Worship in Israel*, pp. 10 ff.

V. HOSEA AS BEARER OF THE WORD

1. The problem is posed by James Muilenburg: "That there are conventional forms goes without saying, and it is important to see that (especially as many do not see it at all), but the conventional is not everything. If it were, all we should have in the Old Testament would be stereotypes, but this we do not have" (private communication). This concern is at the center of Georg Fohrer's critique of current scholarship, "Remarks on Modern Interpretation of the Prophets," *JBL*, December 1961, pp. 309 ff. Though Reventlow, *Liturgie und Prophetisches Ich bei Jeremia*, pp. 15 ff., makes a good case in response to Fohrer, he by no means disposes of the problem.

2. This is especially true of the study of Hosea and Jeremiah. Thus, for example, Artur Weiser, *The Old Testament: Its Formation and Development* (New York: Association Press, 1961), pp. 236 f., and Pfeiffer, *Introduction to the Old Testament*, p. 571.

3. See especially Kraus, *Die prophetische Verkündigung des Rechts in Israel*, and Murray Newman, "The Prophetic Call of Samuel," in *Israel's Prophetic Heritage*, pp. 86 ff., as representative of a growing literature on the subject.

4. Von Rad, *Old Testament Theology*, Vol. II, pp. 75-79.

5. See the discussion among scholars on this very point as Biblical scholars seek a responsible relation to their church traditions. G. E. Wright, "Biblical Studies: Record and Interpretation," *Ecumenical Dialogue at Harvard*, edited by Samuel H. Miller and G. Ernest Wright (Cambridge: Harvard University Press, 1964), pp. 304 ff.

6. Here we assume that the marriage narrative is in some sense historical. See the various options in H. H. Rowley, "The Marriage of Hosea," *BJRL*, September 1956, pp. 200 ff. Thus it is possible that the image came to be used by the prophet because of his own experience. G. E. Wright, "The Terminology of Old Testament Religion," *JNES* 1942, p. 406, writes: "In spite of attempts to the contrary no definite Canaanite background can be found for this unusual conception, and its introduction may still best be explained as due to some peculiar marital (and/or emotional?) experience of Hosea." While stressing the historical dimension, it should be noted that the historical experience may well utilize a conventional image.

7. Worth noting are the affinities to Deut. 8:11, "Take heed lest you forget the LORD your God . . ."

8. This faith had received hymnic expression in the very ancient words of Exod. 15:21 and in the fuller expression, vss. 1-18. It is important to recognize that the very personal expression of the prophet is quite in keeping with the more broadly historical proclamation of the old tradition.

9. The analysis of this material by Wolff, *Dodekapropheton 1, BK,* 14, pp. 35 ff., is extremely helpful, and my discussion is much indebted to it. However, Wolff does not regard the verses as a unit. He regards vss. 2-15 as a unit, vss. 18-23 as a collection of fragments. Against Wolff, our analysis offers evidence for treating the whole as a unit. For a defense of unity, see Hans Lubsczyk, *Der Auszug Israels aus Aegypten,* pp. 19 ff. Paul Humbert, "la logique de la perspective nomade chez Osee et l'unite d'Osee 2, 4-22," *BZAW* 1925 (41), pp. 158 ff., affirms the unity of vss. 2-20, but rejects vss. 21-23 as later.

10. Curt Kuhl, "Neue Dokumente zum Verständnis von Hosea 2:4-15," *ZAW* 1934, pp. 102 ff., and Cyrus H. Gordon, "Hos. 2:4-5 in the Light of New Semitic Inscriptions," *ZAW* 1936, pp. 277 ff., have shown how common legal practice stands behind this formula, which corresponds to non-Biblical parallels.

11. RSV most often renders the particle "for" in this chapter, but that is too weak to catch the rhetorical power of the term.

12. See Lubsczyk, *op. cit.,* pp. 28 f., on the problem of the gods as it is related to the Exodus motif.

13. The crucial conjunction "lest" shows that the entire unit is based on the premise that Israel will not repent as suggested in vs. 2c. So it proceeds in light of the indictment of vs. 2ab. For a like use of the same conjunction, see Deut. 12:30.

14. Gordon, *op. cit.,* and Kuhl, *op. cit.,* show that sending a woman out naked was a practice not unrelated to divorce proceedings. This makes the threat more powerful, for the same language can be used of community humiliation and exile; see Isa. 47.

15. See Hillers, *op. cit.,* p. 23, for the motif in ancient Near Eastern curses and an inversion of the curse in Isa. 55:13. Though the wording is dissimilar, the parallel of Gen. 3:18 is illuminating for both passages.

16. The same verb "remove" is used in Gen. 35:2. Alt, "Die Wallfahrt von Sichem Nach Bethel," *KS,* I, pp. 79 ff., has suggested that this passage refers to a ritual act of renunciation of the foreign gods. The recurring use of the verb may suggest the intersection of ritual and covenantal repentance; i.e., the ritual dramatizes what Israel intends for the covenant relationship.

17. J. Wijngaards, "Death and Resurrection in Covenantal Context (Hos. vi 2)," *VT,* April 1967, pp. 226 ff., has clearly shown that the term refers to embrace of a covenant suzerain.

18. Lubsczyk, *op. cit.,* offers a great deal of evidence to show how the Exodus theme gives focus for a variety of images and motifs.

19. See the work of Begrich, "Das Priesterliche Heilsorakel," *ZAW* 1934, pp. 217 ff., and Westermann, "The Way of the Promise Through the Old Testament," *The Old Testament and Christian Faith,* ed. by Bernhard W. Anderson, pp. 200 ff.

20. Lubsczyk, *op. cit.,* p. 23, suggests that the reference to the Valley of Achor in vs. 15 refers to the purification of Israel by the blood of Achan (Joshua 7:20-26), whereby restored relation with Yahweh was possible. This use of the tradition suggests that Yahweh's new act of graciousness has as its counterpart the purification of Israel; this, of course, is closely related to

the repentance motif in vss. 2c and 7. On the importance of the wilderness theme, see Humbert, *op. cit.*

21. Again the verb "put away."

22. The counterpart in 4:3 has two of the same members in a triad. In 4:3, we see the undoing of creation in curse; in 2:18, the restoration of creation as a blessing.

23. The motif is clearly expressed in Ps. 46:9 in what is perhaps an enthronement hymn, a festival which Mowinckel understands to be a time of covenant renewal. This parallel is important, because it is likely that Hosea 2 is also a liturgic piece for purposes of covenant renewal.

24. Gunnar Östborn, *Yahweh and Baal* (Lund: C. W. K. Gleerup, 1956), p. 72, interprets the term in covenantal terms, "One party says 'yes' to the will of the other." A. Guillaume, "A note on Hosea II 23, 24 (21, 22)," *JTS*, April 1964, pp. 57 f., following the Targum, suggests that the term has the connotation of "it flowed," "let the water escape," "the waterskin leaked"; and so "send down rain" is justified. It is, he concludes, to be read in the causitive, so that it refers to making the rain come and causing the land to be fruitful.

25. Cf. Mowinckel, *The Psalms in Israel's Worship* (Oxford: Basil Blackwell, 1962), Vol. I, pp. 217 ff.; Vol. II, pp. 58 ff.

26. Rather than arguing that these are fragments later put together, as Wolff does, we may note the chiastic structure of the whole.

27. On this total renewal, which is the giving of "wholeness" first delineated in the covenant blessings, see J. J. Stamm and H. Bietenhard, *Der Weltfriede im Alten und Neuen Testament*, p. 43, and *passim*. Östborn, *op. cit.*, pp. 71 ff., in this context speaks of Yahweh as "the God of harmony."

28. The life/death dimensions of covenant breaking and covenant renewal are clear in light of the paper by Wijngaards, *op. cit.*

29. Wolff, *Dodekapropheton I, Hosea*, pp. 39, 58, suggests that vss. 2-15 are soon after 750 B.C., and vss. 16-23 are later.

30. The sojourn tradition as utilized in 2:14-15 regards that early period as one of purity, later championed by the Rechabites (see Jer. 35). As such it is the very antithesis of Canaanite syncretism through which fertility becomes prominent.

31. See my discussion in "Tradition Engaged with Crisis," *Theology and Life*, Summer 1966, pp. 118 ff., on this way of handling tradition.

32. See especially the analysis of von Rad, *Old Testament Theology*, Vol. I, pp. 15 ff.

33. See Östborn, *Yahweh and Baal*, as well as the historical accounts of John Bright, *A History of Israel* (Philadelphia: The Westminster Press, 1959), pp. 234 ff., and Martin Noth, *The History of Israel* (New York: Harper & Brothers, 1958), pp. 253 ff.

34. This is an important reason why scholars have treated prophetic units in a fragmentary way. We have so stressed the "historical factor" that each verse must be related to a historical event. Since passages like 2:2-13 and 2:14-23 cannot be linked to the same historical situation, they cannot be regarded as a unit. This distortion is a result of disregard for the dramatic, liturgical factor in the prophet's words.

35. This is assumed in the analysis of the communal lament which begins

in a mood of despair and moves to a mood of confident faith. In contemporary liturgy, the same movement is experienced in "confession of sin" and "assurance of pardon."

VI. PROPHETIC MINISTRY IN OUR OWN SITUATION

1. The rite and sacrament of ordination characteristically include the prophetic function. It is in the nature of the "office" to permit and recognize charismatic freedom and authority.

2. The claim of Paul (2 Cor. 4:5) is quite in keeping with the prophetic investment in the tradition of faith.

3. This is in keeping with the "symbolic actions" of the prophets whereby what they did had a special power to communicate and initiate new events. See the discussion of H. Wheeler Robinson, "Prophetic Symbolism," *Old Testament Essays* (London: C. Griffin, 1927), pp. 1-7, and his summary in *Inspiration and Revelation in the Old Testament* (Oxford: Oxford University Press, 1946), pp. 185 f., and the study of G. Fohrer, "Die Gattung der Berichte über symbolische handlungen der Propheten," *Studien zur Alttestamentlichen Prophetie (1949-1965)*, pp. 92 ff. On our body (person) as a "word" in history, see Jacques Sarano, *The Meaning of the Body* (Philadelphia: The Westminster Press, 1966), pp. 117 f., 141 f.

4. On the meaning of this whole cluster of words, we still have no better discussion than J. Pedersen, *Israel I-II*, pp. 99 ff.

5. To see the present in terms of the involvement of Yahweh immediately leads one to consider the "new thing" which Yahweh is about to do (Isa. 43:18-19). See von Rad, *Old Testament Theology*, Vol. II, pp. 243 ff., and the studies of C. R. North and A. Bentzen cited there. The prophet discerns in the present the new deed of God which makes even the old celebrated deeds look less important.

6. On the use of the Exodus motif in Second Isaiah see B. W. Anderson, "Exodus Typology in Second Isaiah," *Israel's Prophetic Heritage*, ed. by Bernhard W. Anderson and Walter Harrelson (New York: Harper & Brothers, 1962), pp. 177 ff.

7. There can be no doubt that Jesus functioned in a prophetic role. See John Knox, *The Death of Christ* (Nashville: Abingdon Press, 1958), pp. 112 ff. By this I do not suggest that he was "only" a prophet or "merely" a prophet, as if this were "mere." But this lies beyond the scope of the present discussion. Recently Reginald H. Fuller, *The Foundations of New Testament Christology* (New York: Charles Scribner's Sons, 1965), pp. 46 ff., has reviewed the data with special attention to the eschatological dimensions of the prophetic understanding of Jesus.

8. Rudolf Bultmann, *Theology of the New Testament*, Vol. I (New York: Charles Scribner's Sons, 1951), pp. 11 ff., in his section "Jesus' Interpretation of the Demand of God," has made this point clearly.

9. The Fourth Gospel also takes up the problem. The stress on some form of continuity with the tradition is clear in John 7-8 and especially in 5:46: "If you believed Moses, you would believe me, for he wrote of me."

10. This is an extremely complex problem. But it is clear that the problem of Torah is closely related to the validity of the tradition and that the attitude of the New Testament obviously is not an unambiguous dismissal of

the tradition. On the Torah see G. Barth, "Matthew's Understanding of the Law," *Tradition and Interpretation in Matthew,* by Günther Bornkamm, Gerhard Barth, and Heinz Joachim Held (Philadelphia: The Westminster Press, 1963), pp. 58 ff.

11. The intricate combination of new and old is reflected in the antithetical sayings of the Sermon on the Mount, Matt. 5:21-48. Bultmann, *op. cit.,* p. 13, stresses the newness, but it is also clear that the newness makes sense only as it stands in a close and positive relation to the old.

12. The incident of the temple cleansing (Mark 11:17) is, of course, understood according to the tradition, as the text relies upon old texts (Isa. 56:7; Jer. 7:11).

13. See Matt. 16:2-3; Luke 12:54-56. Jesus' controversy with his enemies and every prophetic controversy is derived from his different discernment of the situation.

14. "The Real Meaning of Law and Order," *Detroit Free Press,* March 14, 1967.

15. Robert Theobald, "Education for a New Time," *United Church of Christ—Council for Higher Education Journal,* March 1967, p. 3.

16. John Kenneth Galbraith, *The Affluent Society* (Boston: Houghton Mifflin Co., 1958) and J. K. Galbraith and M. S. Randhama, *The New Industrial State* (Houghton Mifflin Co., 1967). Joseph Fletcher, *Moral Responsibility* (Philadelphia: The Westminster Press, 1967), pp. 182 ff., has explored the same issue from the perspective of Christian faith.

17. The crisis in the life of an individual may be most dramatic in leaving home and going away to the university. On a larger scale the same crisis is now faced by the whole church community in the process of urbanization.

18. A most comprehensive statement of humanness through the emerging technological civilization is offered by A. Th. van Leeuwen, *Christianity in World History* (London: Edinburgh House Press, 1964). For a quite opposite view see Jacques Ellul, *The Technological Society* (New York: Alfred A. Knopf, 1964); he stresses the demonic power of the new "scientific" apparatus.

19. The fully human person is a theme much explored currently by theologians of the secular. See Larry E. Shiner, *The Secularization of History* (Nashville: Abingdon Press, 1966), and the very important essay by Emmanuel G. Mesthene, "Technology and Religion," *Theology Today,* January 1967, pp. 481-495. The theme is prominent in Bonhoeffer's thought and has been dealt with in another form by Ignazio Silone, *Bread and Wine* (New York: Harper & Brothers, 1937). On the latter, see Myron B. Bloy, Jr., *The Crisis of Cultural Change* (New York: The Seabury Press, 1965), pp. 113 ff.

20. The classical motif in Reformation theology has received no more potent expression than in the thought of Dietrich Bonhoeffer. See, for example, *The Cost of Discipleship* (London: SCM Press Ltd., 1959), pp. 76 ff. The phrase "man for others" is associated with Bonhoeffer.

21. Paul Tillich, *Systematic Theology* (Chicago: University of Chicago Press, 1963), Vol. III, pp. 67 ff., has discussed the work of the Spirit in life in terms of the realization of "humanity" and "justice." His comments there on the human are pertinent to the characterization above.

22. The gospel against demonic forces has been variously illuminated by Tillich, *loc. cit.*, and James M. Robinson, *The Problem of History in Mark* (Naperville, Ill.: Alec R. Allenson, Inc., 1957), pp. 33 ff.; see also Erich Fromm, *You Shall Be as Gods* (New York: Holt, Rinehart and Winston, 1966), pp. 43 ff. It is obviously the counter theme to the emergence of the human.

23. See H. Richard Niebuhr, *The Responsible Self* (New York: Harper & Row, 1963), pp. 142 ff., on the ethics of death.

24. In a quite different context, Aarne Siirala, *The Voice of Illness* (Philadelphia: Fortress Press, 1964), has written about the prophetic as one dimension of healing along with the symbolic. Obviously our perverted understanding of prophecy which "tells people off" is hardly calculated to heal.

25. This characteristic prophetic responsibility is evident in many texts, nowhere more clearly than in Ezek. 18.

26. The prophetic dimension of the New Testament Church is attested particularly in 1 Cor. 12, 14. While it is not stated that every person is a prophet, the intimate connection betweeen community and prophet is clear. H. A. Guy, *New Testament Prophecy* (London: The Epworth Press, 1947), pp. 104 ff., in summarizing the evidence writes: "The prophets exercised their powers in the Christian meeting (I Corinthians 14:16, 23, 26 ff.) . . . The prophet is one who 'builds up' the Church (14:4 f.)." On p. 111, he refers to prophets as "persons of insight," a function quite in keeping with our analysis above. In an older study, Erich Fascher, *Prophetes, Eine sprachund religionsgeschichtliche Untersuchung,* p. 185, speaks of the New Testament prophet and says, "He knows and sees more than the others."

In a study of the contemporary situation, concerning the prophetic function in the church, Gibson Winter, *The New Creation as Metropolis* (New York: The Macmillan Company, 1963), has used the very suggestive phrase, "The prophetic-reflective community." In the present study we have not examined the orientation to the future of which Winter makes much. This is an urgent matter in Scripture study. But Winter's stress on the future has led him to minimize if not caricature the importance of the tradition.

27. Paul Tournier, *The Meaning of Persons* (New York: Harper & Brothers, 1957), p. 200, says, "To live is to choose. It is through the making of successive and resolute choices that man traces out his life."

28. The life of Dietrich Bonhoeffer makes the point.

29. This motif is well expressed in Israel's tent theology, which resisted the domestication of Yahweh in a temple edifice; see 2 Samuel 7:4-6. The issue is not the type of structure but the assumptions about Yahweh's relation to all kinds of human structures and constructions. This tradition affirms that he is always Lord over the structures and is never subordinated to and controlled by them.

30. Emmanuel G. Mesthene, "Learning to Live with Science," *Saturday Review,* July 17, 1965, p. 17.

31. Barry Commoner, *Science and Survival* (New York: Viking Press, 1966), offers a summons to precisely that responsibility.

32. Emmanuel G. Mesthene, "What Modern Science Offers the Church," *Saturday Review,* November 19, 1966, p. 31.

33. Saul D. Alinsky has now brought this to spectacular expression. See his "Of Means and Ends," *Union Seminary Quarterly Review*, January 1967, pp. 107 ff.

34. Again Alinsky, *op. cit.*, has clarified the point. Norman Gottwald, *All the Kingdoms of the Earth*, pp. 365 ff., and *passim*, has investigated the prophetic investment in places where important issues must be faced.